Under the Bed

Stephanie Radok is an artist and writer based in Adelaide on Kaurna land. Her artwork is held in the collections of the National Gallery of Australia, the National Gallery of Victoria, Flinders University Museum of Art, Geelong Gallery and the Art Gallery of South Australia.

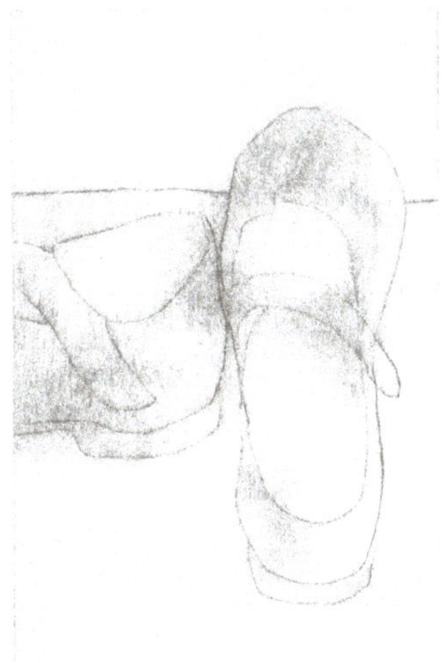

Also by Stephanie Radok

An Opening: Twelve love stories about art

Becoming a Bird: Untold stories about art

Julie Blyfield (with Dick Richards)

Under the Bed

Inventories
2020–2022

STEPHANIE RADOK

with 36 etchings by the author

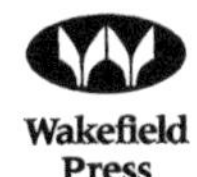

Wakefield Press
16 Rose Street
Mile End
South Australia 5031
www.wakefieldpress.com.au

First published 2025

Edited by Julia Beaven, Wakefield Press
Designed and typeset by Michael Deves
Photography of artworks by Michal Kluvanek

ISBN 978 1 92338 802 4

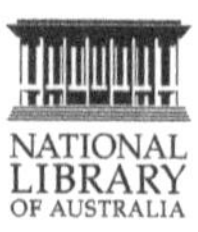

A catalogue record for this book is available from the National Library of Australia

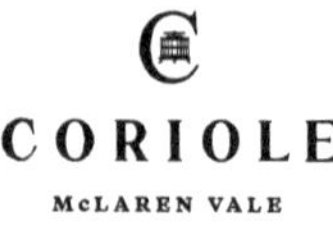

Wakefield Press thanks Coriole Vineyards for continued support

For Jerome with love

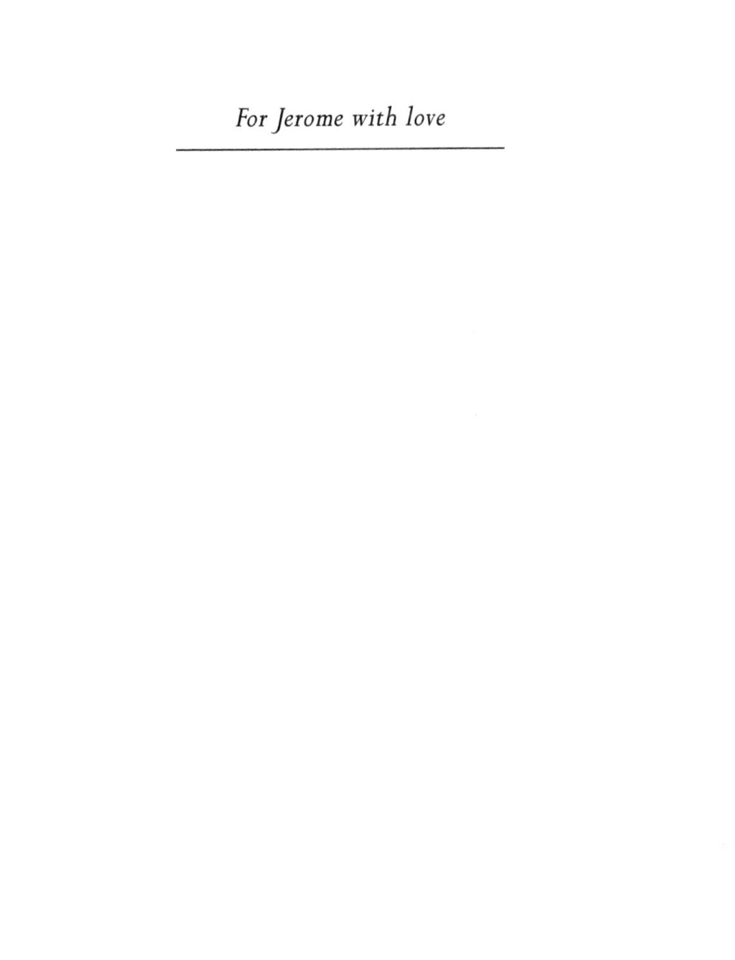

The only dream worth having is to dream that you will live while you are alive, and die only when you are dead.

Arundhati Roy, *The End of Imagination*

The gardener digs in another time, without past or future, beginning or end... As you walk in the garden you pass into this time – the moment of entering can never be remembered.

Derek Jarman, *Modern Nature*

Contents

INVENTORY 2022

Under the Bed

TODAY I WATERED the front garden by hand. Maybe not the most efficient method but efficiency has its limits. I decided to pick three long stalks of feverfew daisies growing near the nectarine tree as they had started to lie down. They have an intense and complex scent half-mint half-chrysanthemum. It is an insect-repelling herb.

I said to the dog, the garden is giving us flowers. And as I held them in front of me and walked towards the mirror in the front hall I was reminded of the artist Paula Modersohn Becker who painted herself several times holding flowers in front of her.

It felt ceremonial and I found my camera, pushed the flowers into the front of my shirt and took a few photos. It was a kind of homage. Both to my mother, who loved to place flowers in vases, and to Modersohn-Becker who died at thirty-one after childbirth, and was a friend of poet Rainer Maria Rilke after whom my father was named. It was for them too.

Rilke wrote a prose work dedicated to her called *Requiem for a Friend* in which, in a translation by Stephen Mitchell, appear the words:

You had just one desire: a years-long work –
which was not finished, in spite of all your efforts.
If you are still here with me, if in this darkness
there is still some place where your spirit resonates
on the shallow sound-waves stirred up by my voice:
hear me: help me. We can so easily
slip back from what we have struggled to attain,
abruptly, into a life we never wanted;
can find ourselves entangled, as in a dream,
and die there, without ever waking up.

Ah Rilke and ah the work. The groping, the plans, the reality, and yet how to begin and how to go on. The what and the why and the who for and the how all rise up towards the solitary artist or writer asking them so many questions and providing so few answers. A years-long work.

There are the interruptions of domesticity, of what we tell ourselves, and what we make ourselves believe, especially for women who often like to give and make life better or at least good for those around them. Feminist icon Ann Newmarch often spoke of interrupted time as a mother and artist and that is, in some way, what Rilke is also describing, the dream of continuity versus the reality of daily life, and all its ways of breaking up the day. Before she died I asked Newmarch for the origin of the resonant quotation that she used in a print in 1975: *We must risk unlearning all the things that have kept us alive for so long*. But she told me that she could not remember.

The rosemary is full of blue flowers. The purple native hibiscus is flowering. The jade tree is covered in mounds of pale pink stars.

In the blue gum hanging over the back fence a koala, a rounded Buddha, a clot of grey in the sky, sits and watches, eats and drops brown scats. On a wet day its ears are like the soft grey-white fluffy heads of dandelions.

Even though some yellow leaves are still hanging on trees and vines new buds are already forming everywhere. The glory vine has delicate green and pink buds starting out of dry sticks. This means if I prune it now it will drip clear sap like tears for a day or two. So, the sap is rising, there is no real downtime in the lives of the trees and other plants but constant movement from one state to another.

The garden is also full of soursobs, bright green and acid yellow. You are supposed to wait until they are flowering before pulling them up and the hope is that their brown bulbs will come out at the same time, which they do, sometimes. The yellow jasmine is also flowering while the buds on the pink one are increasing in size every day.

The snowdrops are starting to come out. I used to think they were the only flowers in the world with green on them and that they had no perfume but when you pick their white bells and bring them inside after a while you notice their scent which is like a liqueur, fragrant and volatile. And the japonica is out, orange and spiky.

On the way to the playground at the top of the street, where the dog and I go almost every day to play ball, there is a small eucalyptus on which hang about fifty chrysalises made from pieces of torn leaves placed together to form what look like tiny pine cones. Like the koalas they are camouflaged. They must have been made by caterpillars. Some of them look quite dry while others are fresher. They have an Egyptian or Mesopotamian quality to them and also a Christmas bauble feeling. One day soon I am going to bring a small branch home so that I can find out what creature they are housing. If I had an old aquarium I would put them in there but might find a vase to hang it in instead.

And I realise that I am something like one of these invisible creatures and have built a layered home around myself of books, a garden, art, and perhaps most valuable of all – pieces of paper on which vital words wait to be followed through or placed with others.

Drops of water hang in all the trees and bushes, evenly spaced on the crab-apple tree branches, in nets on the casuarina, and as shining lights all over the lacy fennel and daisy leaves. Writing is like embroidering with threads taken from the world and from thought, beads of insight, fragments of flowers and seeds, as well as lots of dust that has accumulated and holds time in its imperceptible motion.

In the middle of the night, around four a.m., sometimes/often/but not always, a bird sings a four-note song at intervals. It doesn't wake me up but as I lie there I hear it and imagine it is letting all the other birds and the rest of us know that all is well. Morning is coming.

What shall I do? How often do I open my hands and hold them out to the night? Calling the stars to witness. As a gesture in solitude it has some drama ... and could even be called Rilkean.

A years-long work. There is a kind of archive fever around me – stumbling over piles of my own past, notes, images, objects, I also encounter the pasts of others, people all over the world, family and friends, streaming away in all directions. When I leave the house and go to the market I see stories piled up in every face, every encounter, every piece of clothing, every smile. The idea of treasures, of gifts for the future, folded inside the archives, is, for me, one large reason they exist. Yet getting them out needs more than a systematic mind or indeed a system because an organic archive leaks away in all directions.

I sit on my bedroom floor surrounded by notebooks of every conceivable size, colour and shape. There is no regimentation in this life, even though it includes making notes and writing – there is no tidy progress, no inventory, no order! Damn. Just a great volume of pages scrawled, written, scribbled. Lists for self-improvement, complaints, dreams (a lot of dreams), visions (quite a few), appointments, plans, events, joy, manifestos, copied out passages from books, anger, drawings, misery, shopping lists and accounts, and here and there a flight of writing, and sometimes a poem or something like one lying on its side, half-dead, half-alive, wondering if it will be pulled out and resuscitated or left there.

Like all artists, writers are self-appointed and must have both very thick and very thin skins: thick to withstand indifference, thin to make their observations, and to find the fine edges of meaning in their languages.

Writing is or can be a consoling voice whether you are the writer or the reader. It can wrap you in a warm hug of solace, not always so much the content as the rhythm, the mood and the sense of a world with a form. Then there is sometimes the feeling of being transported to another place, another level of existence, the home of heightened and intensified sensations.

So, here all around me, are multiple notebooks filled with too much embarrassing nonsense and self-revelation to be safe. No-one must ever see these books. It is imperative for me to stay alive long enough to find and destroy them all.

But first I must identify the treasure in them as those few words may keep me or someone else alive. A sense of duty enters here. In some ways it is a defiant echo of myself as a child. When I learned something off by heart I imagined saving lives by knowing those words. We will murder you all, unless someone knows this poem or song, they would say. I can do it, I would pipe up. Memory as power.

Every now and then a shelf of notebooks that I had forgotten turns up to frighten me. And then I appreciate the common sense of religious rituals that, as a side-effect, include cleaning the entire house. I particularly like the description of the Jewish one of ridding the house of bread before Passover that Claudia Roden describes in her Jewish cookbook. Thus religion can improve hygiene and maybe this is one key to its endurance, as well as a way to remove secrets and trails. But how likely is it, really, that all secrets can be removed? Don't we all need them to give our lives depth?

There are notebooks stacked in an old desk, some in a cupboard, piles in a box or two. They are without labels though some have dates written on their covers from former attempts to impose order and some have bookmarks or dogears marking notable moments. They are museums, libraries, suitcases, vitrines, bookshelves, archives, waste places and storerooms. When I hear about someone using the same type of notebook all their life and clearly dating and filing them as if their existence was a neat shelf of bound journals in a library I feel sad. My notebooks lack such a steady rhythm. Such regularity sounds suffocating anyway – the appeal of the random, the accidental, the chance, the unpredictable, except in the case of breakfast, is surely essential and needed for a life to be alive. Patterns can be found later.

The earliest notebooks are tiny, lined booklets, though there are a few unusual heritage notebooks, resuscitated vintage items discovered in op shops. These are followed by exercise books and something relentless starts to happen here as writing becomes as rewarding, in some way, as living, and must be fulfilled, not for posterity, not as a public work to be polished and published or submitted for publication but as release, as pleasure, as necessity.

There are a few volumes from a bookbinding class I took in Canberra, amazing old-fashioned real proper thick hardcover books – one blue, one red, one gray, stitched, stiff, stout and strong – they will be quite hard to burn but I will give it a go.

Then there are the patterned books that a designer has composed to give life a bit of style and colour. There are books of every description imaginable, cheap and ordinary, spiral-bound, stapled, and plain as so often are my hand-written words, though rampant in their scale. Yet sometimes mesmerising, hypnotic, holding even in the thickness or thinness of their inked letters a flavour of the time and the mood they record. While I did once mix my own ink from red and blue to make purple ink in my Baudelaire days of using a fountain pen, mostly it is black or blue that marks the pages, and I recall the scent of some biros to be spicy and inky. There are at least a dozen red and black Chinese notebooks (from both during and after Mao). Then there are the Moleskines, legendary notebooks, beloved of Bruce Chatwin and others. Shiny or matte black, brown paper plain or red lizard skin, whether handsome or restrained in colouring they remain anonymous as they have no markers on the outside. Here and there is the book too good-looking to use. The notebook destined for emptiness, its beauty holding off revelation, confidences or simple documentation.

Will I ever be able to mine the notebooks and then destroy them? Why don't I just throw them all away? Can I relive the past? Is it safer, quieter, eternal? What is it that makes me keep them and occasionally pull one out to try to recreate something with it? Regret, sadness, longing, ambition? In a way it is like walking in a mysterious museum with always more rooms, dim galleries, doorways receding into infinity, glass vitrines with fruit and seeds from ancient tombs, fragments of china and glass beads from lost civilisations. Is it a huge monument to a pathological self-regard or a simple resource, an old jewellery box, a place of unthreaded moments?

A palace of memory. They are a garden too, old, rather overgrown, neglected, abandoned, wild. And must stay wild. The unpacking must be done privately. Secrecy and tenderness are the passwords/bywords. And the people within are often like closed books, sometimes they open a little. Some people go out, some go in and don't appear again.

The notebooks hang over me like an albatross might, if I had one. All the unspoken words piled up, heaped like earth, compost, weeds, leaves, refuse or fertiliser.

Really I have a deep inclination to just crawl under the bed and hide. I seek oblivion and ecstasy, silence and invisibility. Under the bed there is not much room, it is full of rolled up paintings but I think I can fit. And that is where you might find me, under the bed with the paintings, with my paintings.

Yet in this early spring the sky glows intensely just before dark and I must either watch from a window or go out and stand in the garden breathing and holding the light, letting it colour me in. Tonight I see a new moon and a star representing, to my fond imagining, a woman and her dog. Standing, staying, shining.

Finding the treasure. A years-long work.

Inventory

2020

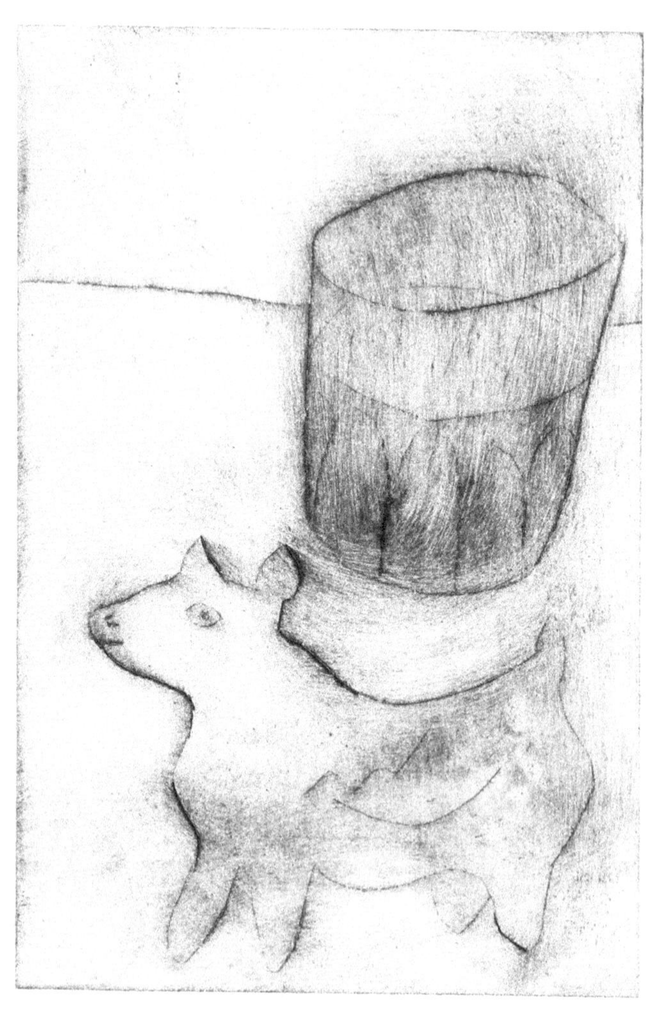

Breathing Space

JANUARY

1
Caught like a child with the alphabet in my hands.

3
The past is very present.

4
A certain structure to a day with the quiet goal of developing own work for own sake and other possibilities.

5
What is kept for memory's sake.

Are there other ways to keep things?

6
Shedding stuff/creating the present/shaping the future.

7
At the beginning of the year or even before, we believe in lists and order, we will grasp the year, and our lives, firmly and conclusively, place it in columns in a book where it can be added up and reviewed, the cost of this, the value of that, the day that something happened. But the year slides in and on like a breeze under a door and refuses to be held.

8
Reading about the lives of others helps us to face our own.

11
Do more drawing. Weed maps again? Inventory – birds, weeds.

12
This side of nowhere – all that I am not.

14
Sometimes we begin at the beginning, sometimes at the furthest point from it.

15
Consider how you spend your time.

18
Last night a green horned bug on the bed, today a terrific matte grey-black beetle at the tank, and a big cockroach on the table. And in the park just when I said to Eno I am seeing creatures everywhere – an owl sitting on the ground at the base of a tree.

20
Are there ceremonies for departing things?

22
Inner toad, inner clown. Haha.

24
A bumper year, a prodigal year/a year of plenty in grapes and quinces.

25
What is this thing they call Covid – a new plague, an epidemic?

Will my street be decimated?

Will the front doors be left open as the bodies are removed and the possums move in?

30
A walk, an excursion, an essay, an exorcism.

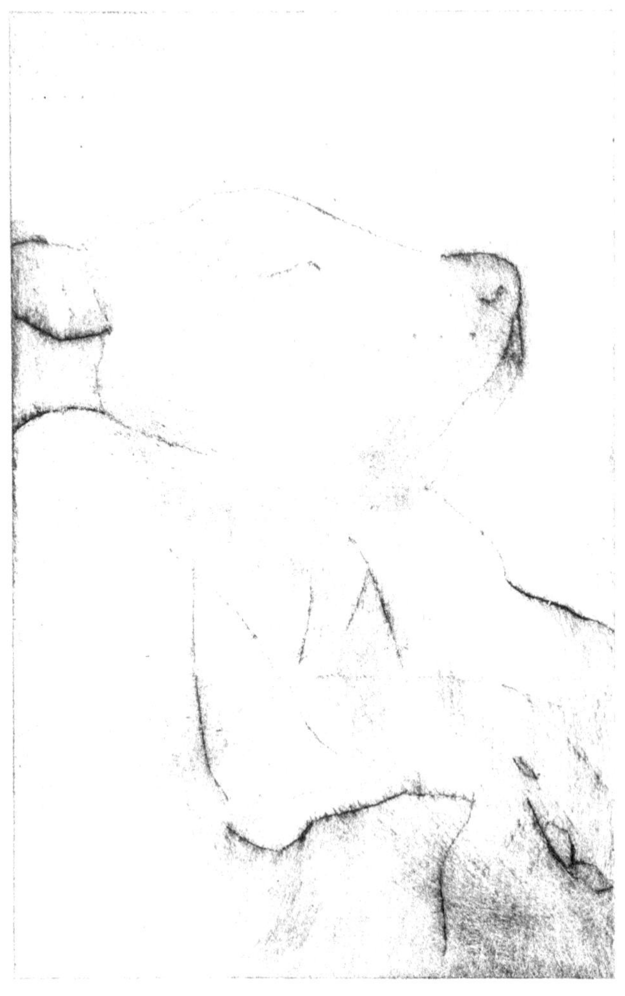

Cathedral

FEBRUARY

2

The dog's breathing is like a cathedral, a forest floor among trees, a shape inside which I can breathe and sleep softly protected from everything. The dog's body is hot like soup. In resting against it a peace enters me that is like the calm sun at noon.

3

There are plenty of words, no shortage of words.

4

We must find our own consolation, constellation. I speak of the sea and each of us being a boat.

5

Don't you love it when you open a book and the words you read connect with a conversation you are having in your head?

7

Competence is the enemy of art. Michelle de Kretser, *The Lost Dog*

9

Every day there is a new reason not to be working. Today it is humidity and the dog.

13

Poverty-garden – of vegetables and herbs – to teach people what their parents might have taught them but didn't. Poverty – about having less, choosing carefully, being thoughtful …

14

I wake up to the scent of the night leaving its sweet darkness, and the words of Nietzsche – *out of chaos you will give birth to a dancing star.* Kookaburras laugh in the distance – *hoohoohaha.* We walk out to see the full moon high in the pale sky, fading stars and clouds full of bears. There is one that looks like you, it looks like you.

15
Being dutiful, devoted, trying to do the right thing.

17
Waldorf salad, red lentil soup with pomegranate molasses, baba ganoush.

18
Invitation to submit a poem to Raining Poetry by 15 March. Theme is Precarity, parameters – no more than four lines, up to fifty characters per line.

19
Aufgabenblatten/Task sheets

I am not learning German but taking bits from memory and reading to sound out. And any other language too. Who owns the words after all?

20
None of us think we will get old. Or die. Tickling stories.

21
Nadie se conoce – Nobody knows himself is an etching from Goya's *Los Caprichos* series. It shows figures in masks and costumes, and refers to the all too frequent self-deception and pretences of people. And indeed to the lack of self-knowledge that we all have.

I love the brevity of the statement. It is tossed off, gloomy, philosophical, bitter.

A trip to the library turns up Robert Hughes' book on Goya where I don't find what I am looking for but find something unexpected and heartening that I haven't encountered before. It's a charcoal drawing of a very old man with long white hair and beard in a long robe and with an alert mouse-like face, probably a self-portrait of the artist, walking carefully with two sticks. In the corner the words *I'm still learning*, in Spanish *Aún Aprendo*. It was made when the artist was around eighty years old.

Apart from his expressive drawing and examination of human folly, tragedy and disaster, it is Goya's use of words to comment in and on his own work that fascinates me. Not limited to pictures the artist speaks, he is sometimes ironic, sometimes poetic. He is a voice as well as an image maker.

He also wrote: *There are no rules in painting.*

21

Hokusai was struck by lightning at fifty and began his life again. Or so the story goes. His famous words describe his life as an artist.

> *From the age of six I had a passion for copying the form of things and since the age of fifty I have published many drawings, yet of all I drew by my seventieth year there is nothing worth taking into account. At seventy-three years I partly understood the structure of animals, birds, insects and fishes, and the life of grasses and plants. And so, at eighty-six I shall progress further; at ninety I shall even further penetrate their secret meaning, and by one hundred I shall perhaps truly have reached the level of the marvellous and divine. When I am one hundred and ten, each dot, each line will possess a life of its own.*

23

What you thought was passing/casual was your life. And a particular red-purple near a blue hillside that seemed to reflect you.

27

Denkbilder/Thought-pictures

Last night in the almost dark I picked a Cécile Brünner rose and saw that a young praying mantis had stepped onto my hand with it. I placed my hand close to the bush so it could step back and it did. Could barely see it but looked again and we exchanged glances before it went on its way. And I remembered when my dad took a photo of a very big one carefully held on my mum's hand and it bit her and she screamed loudly. He always spent a long time focusing when taking photos.

29

My relationship with brush painting started a long time ago when I bought a traditional inkstone, a stick of ink and a bamboo-handled brush at an art supply shop. I went on because it suits me. It is expressive and immediate, drawing and writing together.

I didn't want to be a writer – I was always a writer. I wanted to be a poet, an actor, an artist, but that's another story. From early on my parents said that I must have kissed the Blarney Stone even though they knew I hadn't been to Ireland. My mother's father was Irish but I never met him. Nor did she really.

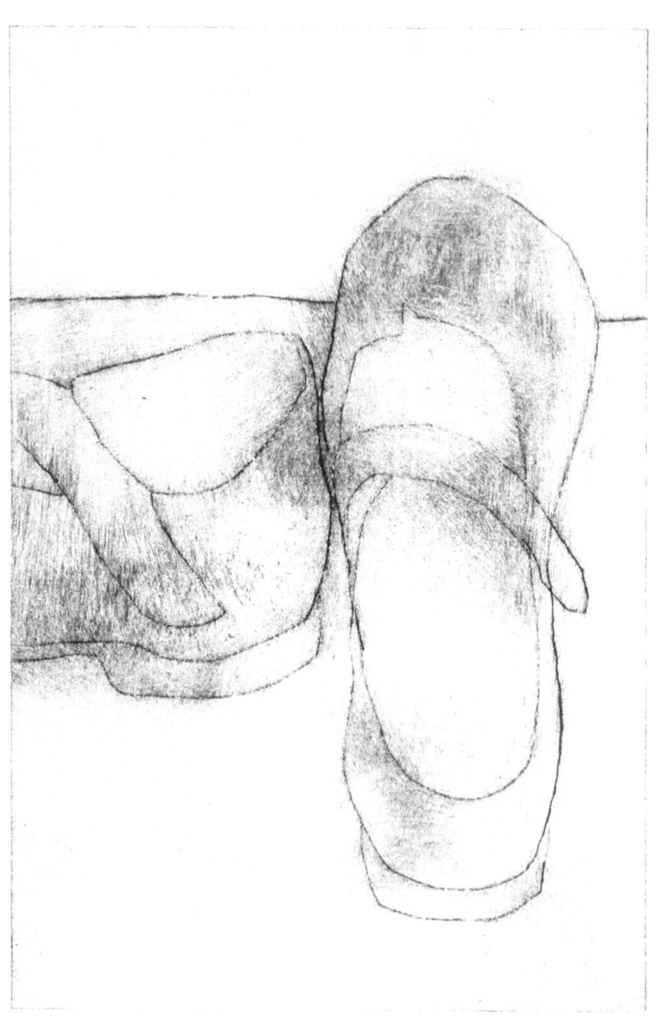

Walking Shoes

MARCH

4

Songs without words. The birds are in the garden watching me. What are they saying? The same things, over and over.

5

We are all on an edge, an edge where we cannot stop. Is there a story, what's the story?

6

The less you have the less you get – superannuation.

7

This is where we begin.

8

Spend more time listening to birds is the title of my etchings of birds in pairs. It is the expressions in their eyes and bodies that are most important. The slightest shift of line or dot moves their faces from surprise to suspicion.

What keeps a bird up in the air is the shape of its wings. Crows and magpies can recognise and remember human faces. Birds have a central role in creation stories and journeys of the soul after death, as mediators between life and death, also as oracles or tricksters.

11

Each of us is as simple as sand, here a look, an eye, there a touch, a word, the eyes touch, the words look, as simple as sand.

13

Fringe concert Steve Reich's *Music for 18 Musicians* at Elder Hall creates a certain space – pulses of sound/thoughts of a life lived/unlived/examined/unexamined.

14

You and your inadequate tail – words for Eno. To think that this, the disregarded everyday, the aggravating dog and his hunger, the chaos of the week, and the world, might one day be precious treasure, a memory of ordinary peace. So I photograph the crowded mantelpiece and the dog with his too short tail, his comma. I sometimes say he is the comma to my sentence. One day we might/I might remember this ordinary day and night as extraordinary, a blessed calm moment of snore and socks and clean sheets and sleep.

15

Beach walk, paddling calm and deep breathing of salt and seaweed air, then bitten by a crab on my right heel! On the way home I buy prawns, fish and calamari to cook.

16

Dream

In an exhibition I take a soft green crayon from my pocket and start drawing on the yellow and white canvas hanging on the wall. I shock myself and stop. I think well no one will know it's me and look at the crayon and put it in my pocket. Then keep walking but also popping back to look at what I have done.

17

We are waves of the same sea, leaves of the same tree, flowers of the same garden. Seneca

These words were written on boxes of masks donated to Italy by China. Quarantined by the epidemic in Italy, people are singing to each other from their balconies. The skies and seas everywhere are empty of people, for a while anyway. This moment of poetry and fellow-feeling and significant change – will it last? The dream of a planet without people.

18
Shelter in place. In time of plague … brightness falls from the air.

In Venice the canals are clear.

19
The trick is – there is no trick.

20
Sometimes it seems as if everything I have done is ragged and half-finished. How to get on and do the secret work.

21
In the cool of the morning – gardening.

A Journal of the Plague Year. I have a fragile ancient copy of this book by Daniel Defoe – is this a good time to finally read it or just think about its title? What needs to be done? What can be done?

22
Doris Lessing's *Memoirs of a Survivor* – is it here somewhere? Will it help?

23
What do you love? What do you long for? The work that you want to make is to be ecstatic and you don't get there through craftsmanship.

24
Painting is an act and all the planning in the world doesn't do it.

25
With Covid we are suddenly thrown into history which we had sort of hoped to avoid. The changes my mother, her mother and her mother lived through were many so why should my life be any different?

26

Dark night of the soul/or the soil. Night soil. Dante – *in the midst of life I came to a dark wood.*

28

Eno likes Bach, he says you say Bark.

29

You might die this year. Are you ready?

Things just got real, very real. People you know might die this year before their time.

Thinking of having a fire and cooking chevapchichi, tzatziki and potato salad. Will the street be like Pompeii – full of empty houses? I haven't seen toilet paper for sale for at least a fortnight.

30

To get through this – reading a first aid book, should attend to advanced care directive. Being mortal – tsk. Knocking on Heaven's Door. Playgrounds – locked gates – how to explain to Eno.

31

There's all that holding back and waiting. And all the letting go that needs to be done. You are not your pain, your past or your emotions. Maybe. Maybe not.

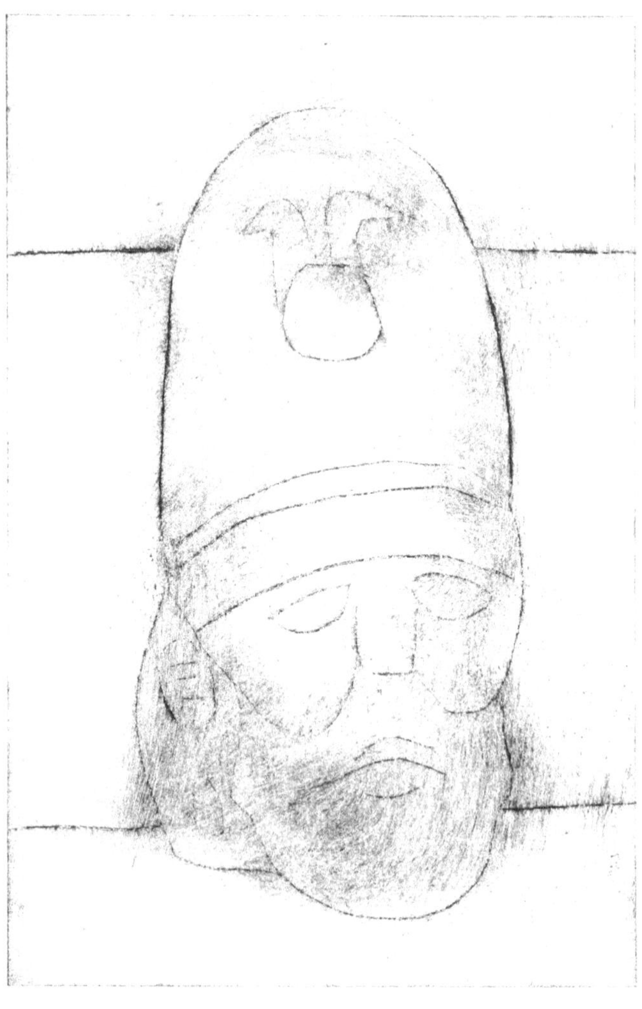

Solomon Islands Mask

APRIL

2
Prepare to die – what needs to be done?

Pea soup, herrings, roast potatoes.

3
I see the importance of doing things with your hands, a balance of thought and sensation. The toilet paper goes in an hour, they say it is delivered to the supermarket at night.

4
Doing vs thinking, body vs mind, or both at once somehow. Dandelions, eggs and bacon.

5
The meaning of the name Radok is joy. Where did I find that? Can't locate it again. Was it a dream? Choir makes me think of school or kindergarten – people's singing faces look as if they are trying to be good, like virtuous children. Should we even be singing in a group?

6
Sometimes a sensation of lightness. What is this moment? Geography – drawing and words. Geo (earth), graphy (drawing). Drawing the earth.

7
Need to eat an apple a day – a carrot too. And look for toilet paper. Eno is training me to never leave him. Roast chicken legs with fennel seeds and potatoes.

The end of the world as we know it in four weeks?! Whew.

8
People are free (almost) to buy all the toilet paper. History herstory are spaces to think. Claude Lévi-Strauss famously said of animals that they are *good to think*. Contrast your own

history/museum with the bigger one. Proofreading is full of thinking. The past is bright in objects – meaning? A lyricism, the writing casts a bit of a spell. Sky-hills.

9

Common sense that's no longer common.

10

Good Friday. Friends around a fire in the backyard, eating, drinking, talking, feeling good. The sky is a white net of clouds.

11

NBN installation. Falafel, tahini, coleslaw.

12

How does a bird stand? Alert – legs wide.

13

Seven impossible tasks. The lists go on and on.

14

Painting is ecstatic – the ecstasy of paint.

15

Roast lamb, garlic, rosemary, honey, potatoes.

Snails are company, companions, consolation.

16

Dream

The toilet is blocked and I must deal with it – I realise I need to probe with the brush and hoick out roll after roll of unused toilet paper.

17

Writing – often cursory, too cursory, sometimes lyrical – using language like paint.

18

We walk up the street, turn the corner and smell water in the air. And collect a monarch butterfly that is somehow stunned but not quite dead. It sends a strong buzz of something like electricity into my hand. The life force. And flies away.

20

A palpable sense of words offering consolation. Trying to recall the origin of a piece of writing, a group of words going round and round in my head, their rhythm like a knot – they speak about a book or an artwork that holds 'such specific character of time and place'. Maybe I will remember it one day.

21

I feel like the garden is wrapping itself around me. I am gently shaping it and it me. Is it more scary to treasure your life or not?

Making artwork that I am calling *Family* – on sheets of thick paper folded in half.

I am using green paint to make rough basic shapes of introduced plants, 206 of them drawn from the 1909 book *Naturalised Flora of South Australia* by J.M. Black. On the side of the page facing the plant I write in red ink the scientific words in the book describing the plants. I write them in layers so they are only partly legible. It is a cacophony, a Babel of meaning, information, knowledge, blood and sap.

And I recall in the National Library of Australia in Canberra many years ago listening to a Hazel de Berg interview with sculptor Robert Klippel where he spoke of making a vocabulary of forms through drawing. And I remember making my notes in tiny writing on tiny pieces of paper, probably on the back of order slips for books. They may even be here somewhere.

22

We are all going to die, that is one thing that makes life precious. With the new disease Covid some will die very quickly, very soon. Is it possible to be ready to die?

Today we see a couple and their dog who has, like David Bowie, one blue eye and one brown one. I ask can the dogs say hello. They say yes he likes to say hello. The dogs' noses touch. Eno cries out. Oh, a talking dog says the woman and starts to say more but goes on walking.

23

Last night I got up at 4 am. While I went to the bathroom Eno rolled himself up in the bedclothes. So then we had to go outside so he could squat in the garden, and I could look at the stars.

24

Gerhard Richter has a big retrospective show at The Met in New York called *Painting After All* that no one can go to as Covid has shut the gallery after nine days. It can be viewed online. Some works are good with red and green blurry flares of paint though too many are dreary cerebral and banal timewasters. Some are made from Auschwitz photos – why do that? Why harp on pain and injustice? Apparently the original photos are on show too.

I have postcards propped up here and there around the house and no less than three are of paintings by Richter. Each bought not because it was by him but because it spoke to me. One postcard is *Grosse Sphinx von Giseh* that reproduces a black-and-white illustration of the Sphinx with a caption. It is like a page torn from a school textbook and was painted in 1964. Another postcard is one that looks like a Polaroid, a big blurry bunch of yellow flowers called *Tulpen* (Tulips) painted in 1995. The third postcard is *Venedig*, which I bought because it reminded me of the edge of the sea in Venice. It was painted in 1985. Eventually by accident I discovered that *Venedig* is the German word for

Venice. That was a day of wonder. It hangs in the kitchen from a thin nail.

24
A dream painting is not a painting.

25
Four years – me and Eno!

26
What have you been doing all these years? Devotion, work, caring. A bird sings a note twice outside the window.

27
As usual I wish I had someone to talk to – someone encouraging and insightful, consoling and far-sighted, brilliant and bold – maybe that is why we write. And read.

28
J's birthday – tofu and noodles and French apple cake.

29
When meditating I recall Canberra in fog – blue and red – white fog lying in the street – Mount Ainslie – hills – Limestone Avenue.

30
When Eno and I get caught in the rain on a walk we come home and run through the house from end to end chasing each other, doing sharp turns, sliding on rugs and getting breathless. Even when we don't get wet we sometimes do it. It reminds me of what my mother told me about a dog they had who used to celebrate when visitors left the house by dancing and seeming to say: they've gone, they've gone!

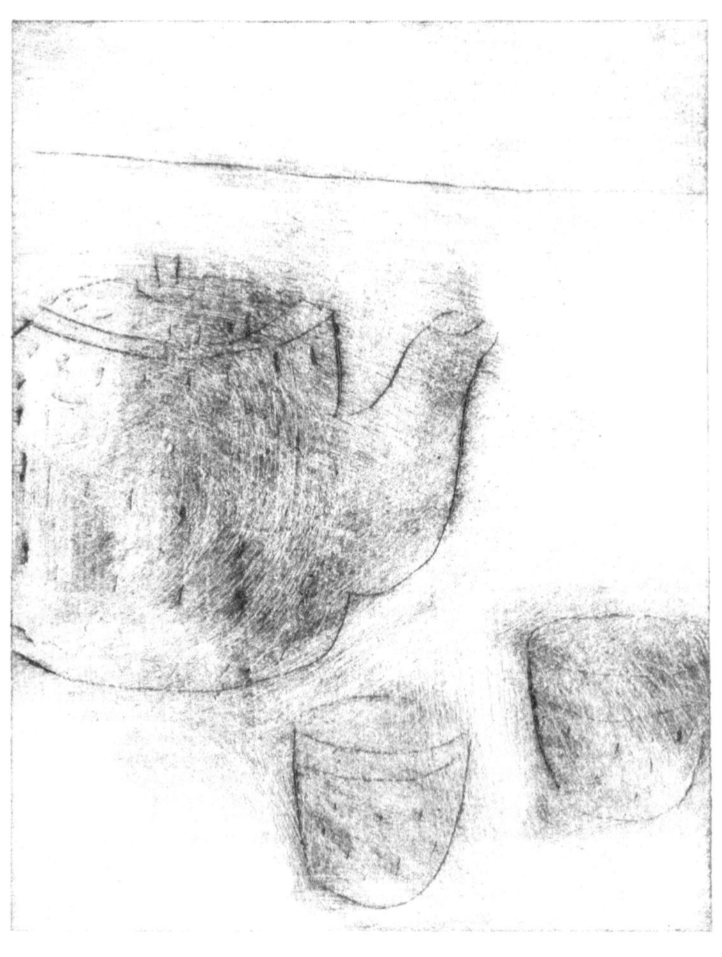

Instant China

MAY

1

Need a plan, even though I avoid them.

2

Developments will happen if you are on the/a road. I guess there is frugality and a sense of recycling/gleaning/immortality in it. Drink more water/do your real work. Are you consistent or monotonous?

3

Leiden – to bear, to endure, to suffer. I first heard the word in a German song about a rose that we learnt as children. *Röslein auf der Heiden* is a song made from a poem by Goethe about seeing a boy who grabbed a rose and was stabbed by its thorn and must then suffer the pain always.

Muss es ewig leiden – must it forever suffer

He must have got tetanus. There's no cure for tetanus!

4

Dream

Large ropes of cobwebs in/over a cupboard/mirrors. I must remove and dispose of them.

5

There is some place where you are and where you aren't.

6

If you have nothing else to love you may as well love a notebook or a colour.

7

The touch and scent of paper and ink. Wordlessness.

8
Essays/manifestoes/dreams/collections/words/weeds/thoughts/aphorisms/epiphanies.

9
Autotelic.

10
Everyone in Australia to be tested for Covid?

11
Things to do in lockdown – not done. Work on my Scottish accent. Learn poems off by heart. Cook new dishes. But I do those things all the time. Well not the accent so much. Och.

12
The voraciousness of reading the screen, the seduction of sleep. Images and words. And music.

13
A peaceful evening in the study. Eno standing under the table like a table.

14
Too much thinking vs not enough doing.

15
The mystery of life is not solved by success, which is an end in itself, but in failure, in perpetual struggle, in becoming. Patrick White, *Voss*

16
Artwork and writing exist over time. When you see them arranged together their recurring features and preoccupations become visible. Made space in studio.

17
Made more space and vacuumed. Feels good, really good.

19
A grain of madness. Necessary, contingent, sufficient.

20
Herb tea, tisane, decoction, infusion, a light touch. Thinking about what to make for the *Medicinal Botanical* exhibition at the Museum of Economic Botany if it happens. There seems some doubt about that – Covid, people moving and so on.

21
Making lists of plants. Plant use – drugs – opium, hemp, kava, tobacco, pituri, mushrooms, tea, coffee. Plant use – fabric – flax, bark.

26
Let food be thy medicine and medicine be thy food. Attributed to Hippocrates.

27
Who you are. Who you are not. Mucking around/not knuckling down/need to be nowhere/come from nothing.

29
Waiting each day for that open space where words fall or colour moves like rain across the sea.

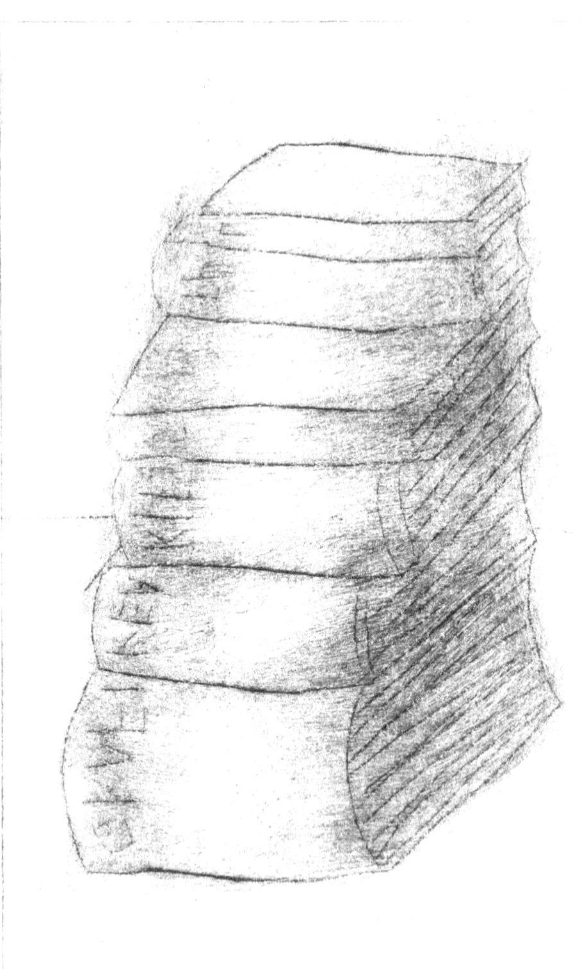

The Great Metaphor of the Book

JUNE

2
The moaning of life. The archaeology of home.

3
Lovely moments last night in backyard on path a snail with long long eyes out on stalks till Eno sniffed it and it withdrew them – later on they were still short. There were two possums in the Liquidambar tree, I thought just one at first but actually two – their ears identical. I waved.

4
People tell stories/make up stories to deal with things/to tell things/to be things.

5
Conversation among friends – to remake the world.

6
To have learnt again that warmth is everything.

8
My birthday. Family dinner.

Du musst dein Leben ändern. Rilke

9
We are all old now, old-looking anyway. Though I still feel at the beginning of everything.

10
Sometimes a sensation of weightlessness comes upon me when I am doing my work. I can see patterns, multiples, words, and enter the world of silent things.

11
Who has ever heard of book lungs in spiders? One of the longest-running controversies in arachnid evolution is whether the

book lung evolved just once in a common ancestor or in several groups as they came onto land. Maybe people too evolved in several groups? I suspect so.

12

I am painting images on paper of fifty foodstuffs – as consumed by me in a week. They are herbs, nuts, fruit and vegetables, and I am making a list of their origins. The work is about an immense daily engagement with botany. In South Australian suburbia food from local farms and from all over the world is delivered and consumed every day. Surely this is miraculous. I will call it *The Museum of Domestic Botany.*

I paint their names in red ink over portraits of the food or its parent plant. They have an educational flash-card language-learning aspect about them. A device for memory, learning and homage. And gratitude for farmers everywhere.

13

For a while I had breakfast with a man who savoured every mouthful with attention and ecstasy. He used to say: *you choose how you live.* I guess this is sometimes true.

The model for *The Museum of Domestic Botany* work is some echo of herbals that throughout the ages combine text and image to identify and instruct.

A medieval inventory – the world as sacred and self-renewing.

14

The bed is a boat, a raft, an ark, and sleep is another country. And the dog is all peace, mostly.

15

The things you think about when painting … best to not think too much of course.

18
When you have been squashed for a long time it can be hard to find your shape.

21
A story of sorts, a story of thoughts.
The great metaphor of the book.

24
Singing was good. Then the silence.

25
Making artworks makes me think again about what it is to make something rather than talk about it – it's all decision/decision/decision. One after the other. And doubt/fear, complex/simple, refined/raw, slow/fast, skilled/loose … alive and engaged in the moment. Artwork – care/caring/careful to be free/to get lost in it. So amazing to research, find and see a sesame plant, a lentil plant.

27
Why collect your history? Why hang on to it? Must you agonise about everything? Always the big picture. Eno and I say to each other – we all want everything to be the same all the time forever. And, by the way, we don't know where anything is.

29
A beautiful day – all silvery yellow and green.

31
My poem sent to the Raining Poetry project was accepted! Along with others the poem is to be spray-painted with hygroscopic paint in the city in August. The poems can only be seen when it rains or you water them. Who knows how long they will last.

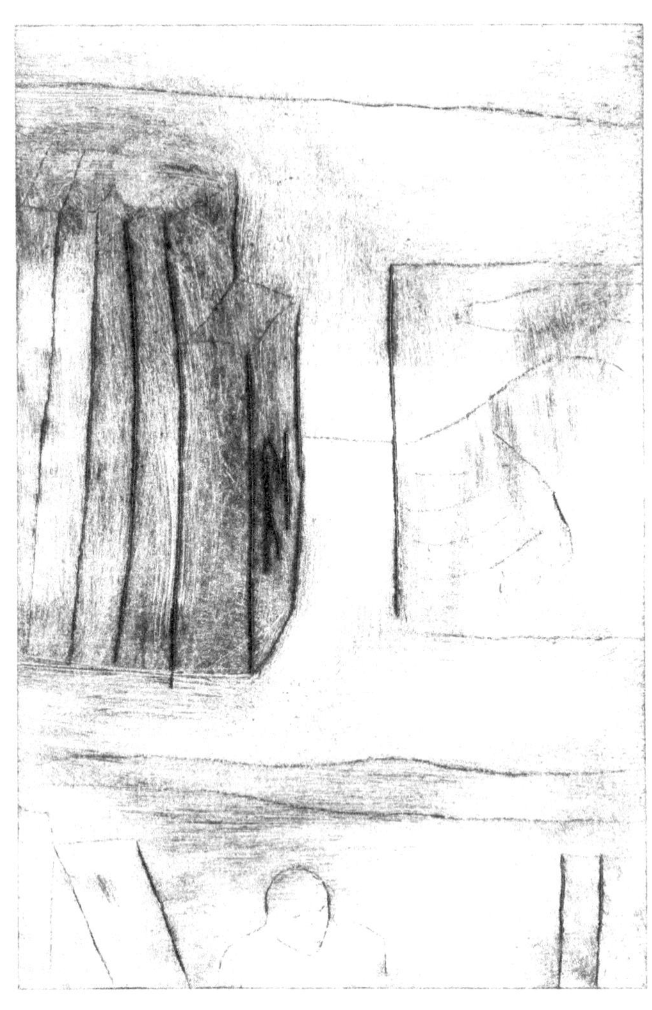

Mantelpiece

JULY

2

Today the sunlight burst in every door and window with a clear calm light, green and softness, silence, leaf-shine and shadow, red stems, yellow leaves, blue flowers.

Maybe because we know a storm is coming it is calmer/quieter/more silent.

3

A koala is wedged in the fork of the blue gum. The storm is coming. The deep dog silence that I adore. Gas, dandruff, whining, it's all okay 'cos there is love.

6

A woman in the park tells us we are not a woman with a dog but a dog with a woman.

I say he is old and also do you think I am spineless? Clearly she does. We walk infinitesimally slowly as I trail along after him, always attached by the lead, pandering while pondering, stopping and starting, letting him call the trail. After all he is the one alert to a hundred thousand scents not me. And I don't want to tell him what to do all the time. I am thinking of other things.

7

Being here with so much old stuff seems odd and I think helps to make me feel that I am still a child.

8

I do a great line in regret, my hands like bird wings.

10

On the mantelpiece I have a postcard of *Tomorrow will be the same but not as this is*, a painting of a river flowing beneath a mountain by Colin McCahon. The words are painted along the bottom edge of it. It's not a quote but his words. Curator and historian Justin Paton says he has seen posters and postcards of it pinned up in many NZ artists' studios.

15

Let me be a lighthouse – words upon my lips on waking.

19

Dream

In a room we are hanging artworks up. We speak of another time the work was shown and he says I have a photo of you from then. Then another friend and I walk and recite *The Second Coming* by Yeats.

20

Buy facemasks – may as well. Make falafel.

24

A book takes you inside … something … someone.

30

A person is like a stone with layers, crystals and colour. A person is like a tree with branches, leaves and fruit. A person is like the sky with clouds, a moon and stars. A person is like a garden with paths, shadows and herbs. A person is like a home with rooms, floors and walls.

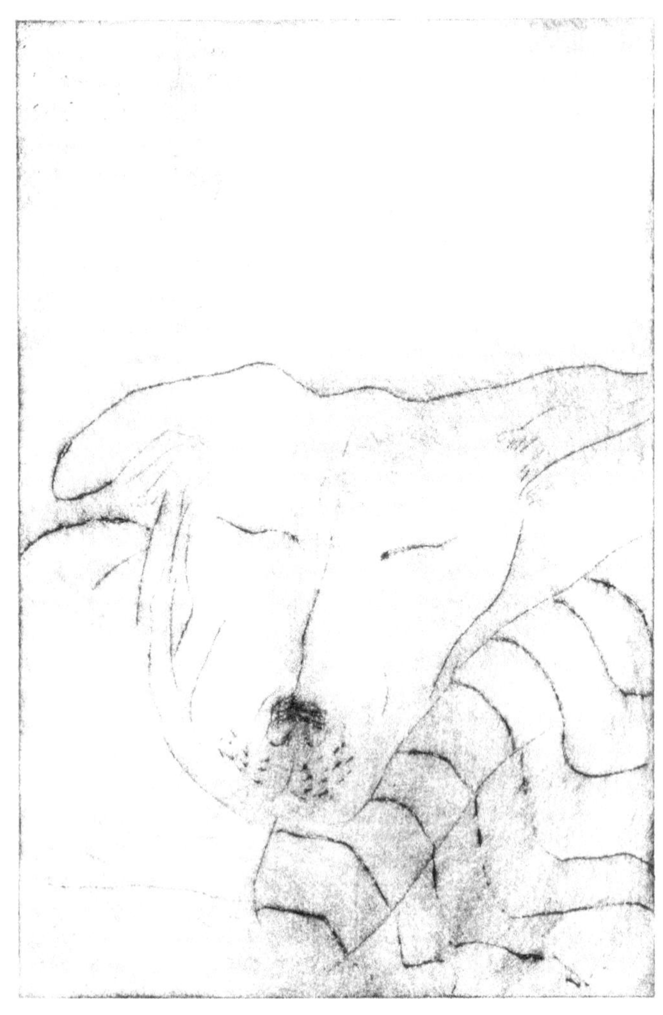

Palace

AUGUST

1

The dew this morning – lots of it scattered on green grass pointing up. I don't want ten thousand fragments. I have ten thousand fragments. I want to form a whole of fragments.

3

Pea soup, fish tagine, baclava.

4

Where the hills go down to the sea.

5

In the long tunnel of the night we make herbal tea and talk about the stars. I think about healing – the world, the house, my life. Your breath is a palace, your eyes are windows.

7

On the news an interview with a man in Beirut after the explosion. He says: *We've lost our home. We've lost our business. We've lost our lives. We're trying to stay positive.*

8

Dream
Rooms in each of which hangs a Hieronymous Bosch work or several in frames. Another room where I keep finding shards of blue-and-white china.

9

Walk at the beach and see dolphins, dolphins.

10

Go love without the help of any Thing on Earth. William Blake

11

Thick description, local knowledge.

13
The gift of Eno. From a distance I can see the purity of his face. He looks wonderful today.

14
Watching Brian Dillon talking about *Essayism* in Shakespeare and Company bookshop in Paris. *An essay doesn't need a conclusion.*

15
Dip and celery, soup, pork chop with plum sauce and vegetables – a three-course meal with Helen Garner's *Diary.*

16
Eno gets me to sit on the sofa with him by standing and staring at me. Pretty tricky.

17
This great silence, a ringing in my ear that seems to consume my brain. You are here to make the inventory of everything, picking the past like flowers. Remember Philip Glass in the movie by Scott Hicks: *Why are we here? We're here to do the work.*

18
The world is wide but my path is narrow. The world moves with a continual flow while I stop and wait, study old books and boxes of flashing ideas, regret and indecision. The world shifts and stirs with blankets of darkness and rain while I arrange objects on shelves which go on to arrange themselves. There is a silent roaring against the window. I try to find my place, to remember where I am, to look after myself and others as well as I can. The sound of the rain, white brushstrokes on loose canvas. The world turns and I follow.

22
Strange times/end times. How many apocalypses can one world have?

24

We are singing and trying to wake neither the dog nor the sleeping children. We are opening the words to the present with our breath and being, stopping time, lighting the dark.

26

I want to catch the flow, the flower of life, to milk it as if it was an old goat and make cheese from it like my sister who wastes no scraps. I am made of rye bread with caraway seeds, dates and yoghourt, apples, honey, and goat cheese too when I am lucky.

28

Drove up in the hills to meet Melinda Rankin, Director of Fabrik at Lobethal. It is an art, culture and history space located in the old Onkaparinga Wool Mill. Here they used to spin sheep's fleece and make blankets and other woollen things.

I told her about the paintings of food plants I have been making and she is interested in exhibiting them in September.

30

My Raining Poetry poem has been sprayed on the pavement island outside Government House. I went in early with the dog and had to borrow cash from someone on the street not realising that you had to pay for parking early on a Sunday morning. Went again with J and this time took a water bottle to sprinkle on the poem to make it visible, grey on grey.

Always knew I was a grasshopper
not an ant
but does the wind
need to be so cold

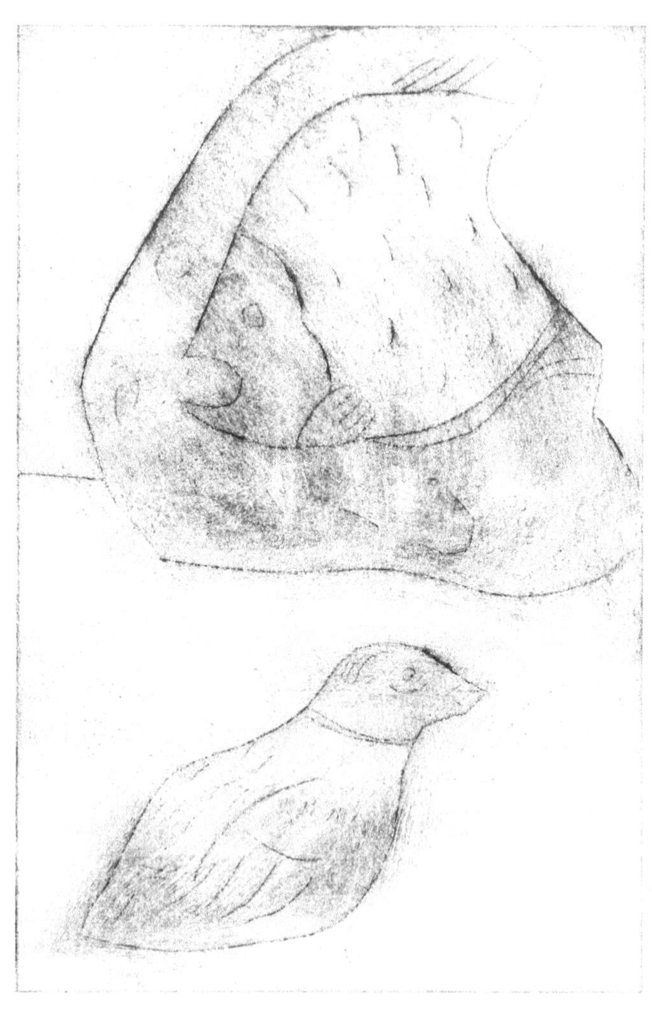

Souvenirs: Bird, Fish

SEPTEMBER

1

Self-knowledge is elusive and maybe also illusory.

5

The hundred things I didn't say.

6

Beach walk hurrah. Two albatrosses. A dog is neither a robot nor an object. Nor am I.

9

Too much self-reflection is as bad as not enough.

10

To see the world in a grain of rice. Handling food – the primal things.

11

Making new work I am calling *Adelaide Wall Paintings* on large pieces of unstretched canvas with a sense of urgency as the show opens this month at Fabrik. Each one is based on a smaller painting on paper or cardboard of part of the garden, very loose, with a sensation of fresco, a light touch. Watery green, blue and bright yellow. And much air to fly through. I did want to paint on the wall but that didn't happen. Fabrik is an industrial space full of light. The canvases will hang beside vitrines full of stacks of my paintings of food plants, old garden tools and my fossil books.

12

Domestic Botany begins in childhood. Garden tools are handed down from generation to generation, or lost amongst the plants.

14

Seeds and stories, memory and imagination, the lives of plants and those of people are joined together in books.

16
The generation of the heart of the world.

18
The thing about spring is its familiarity.

20
Can you write and paint?

Can you think and paint?

Can you write and think?

22
Museums are portals to memory. Fossilised books can no longer be opened but are full of quiet moments of great happiness. It's called reading. A fossil book contradicts a book in that it can't be opened but it can be imagined which is often better.

25
I attend Alan Brissenden's funeral online. He was the best university lecturer I ever had. Words about him … impressive, wide-ranging. He was called a happy sharer, respectful, cheerful, inquisitive. A lively and intelligent man of wit and curiosity who apparently loved eating cheese with a Barossa Valley red, and annually cleaned his chandelier. He has five grandsons. I once gave him a lift home from an *Adelaide Review* launch. He was their dance critic, I was one of their art critics.

26
The exhibition opens at Fabrik. We all have to sit down with our drinks and have paper bags of snacks so that we do not mingle our breath or hands. We are not wearing masks however. It all feels strange and like a subdued emergency. Has life changed forever?

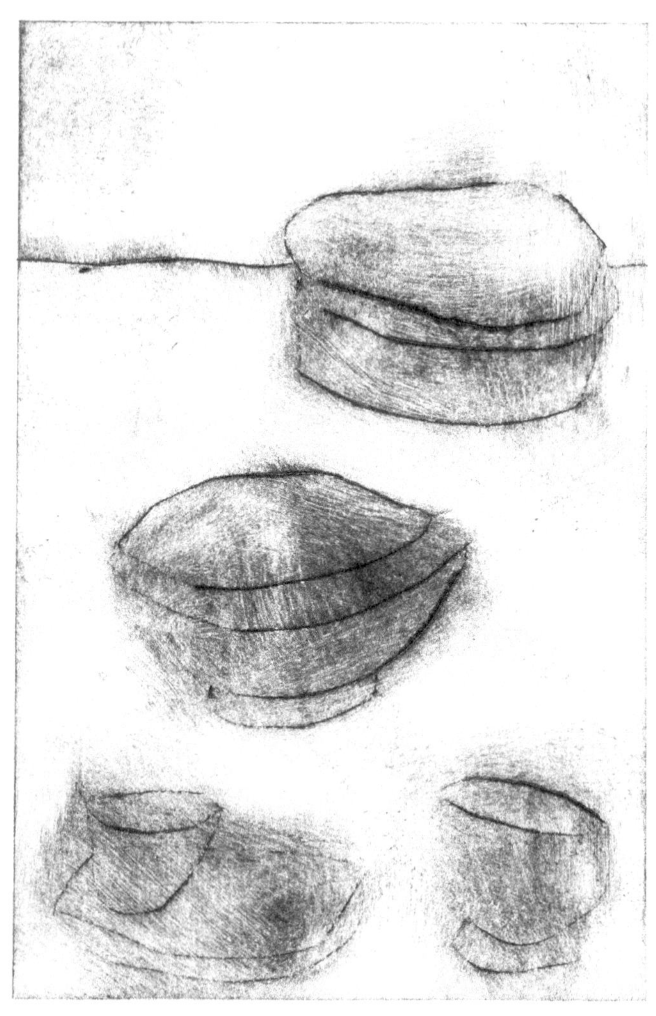

Boxes and Cups

OCTOBER

1

What have I learned from *The Museum of Domestic Botany*. How good it was to make the work, to know it would be seen, to have to make decisions. The importance of not overthinking. To be gentle and thoughtful.

2

Casting off. The gestural work.

3

Epiphany is not only revelation or insight, it is also the reassembly of the self through the senses. Teju Cole

8

Prevarication/oblivion/planning/escapism/provincialism.

9

Black cockatoos – one and a flock. Their languid movement across the sky, their wings, their calls. A lack of solitude, a noticing of solitude.

10

Noetic.

11

My history/versions of it/stopping points/decisions/old drafts.

12

Beginnings are easy. Sticking with something is not easy. For me there needs to be an element of discovery involved.

13

Garden pressing in at every window swelling green and roses.

14

Winnowing, unwinding – writing the same book twice.

15
No internet. Let's call it a hiatus. The air possesses a certain wide silence. I decide to record more about each day. And to seriously at long last make more space around me by sorting and discarding, as well as cleaning and repairing. This is my constant task but really always a prelude.

16
Dream
With an old friend at an exhibition, a circular museum of childhood, and at the top of the stairs you add an apple and it all lights up.

17
Uncovering memories must be combined with embracing the present because retrieval on its own is too heavy a task.

18
Lacrimae rerum – the tears of things. I buy a bottle of Italian dry sparkling wine called Dante. *He* was a writer I say to myself out loud but not too loud in the bottle shop.

19
Through illness a growth in self-knowledge.

20
The light leaving the garden.

23
Cameras without film – the act is there – and there is no tedious product to store or view … this is A Radical Idea.

25
Prawns, roast red capsicums, tabouli.

27
Untold stories are about what – the growth of compassion, of suffering, solitude and privacy. Editing the final proof of

my book. It's charming/clunky, cute/repetitive, rhetorical/unfocused, archaeological/original.

29
Incantation, healing.

30
You and walls and walks. Beijing – Venice.

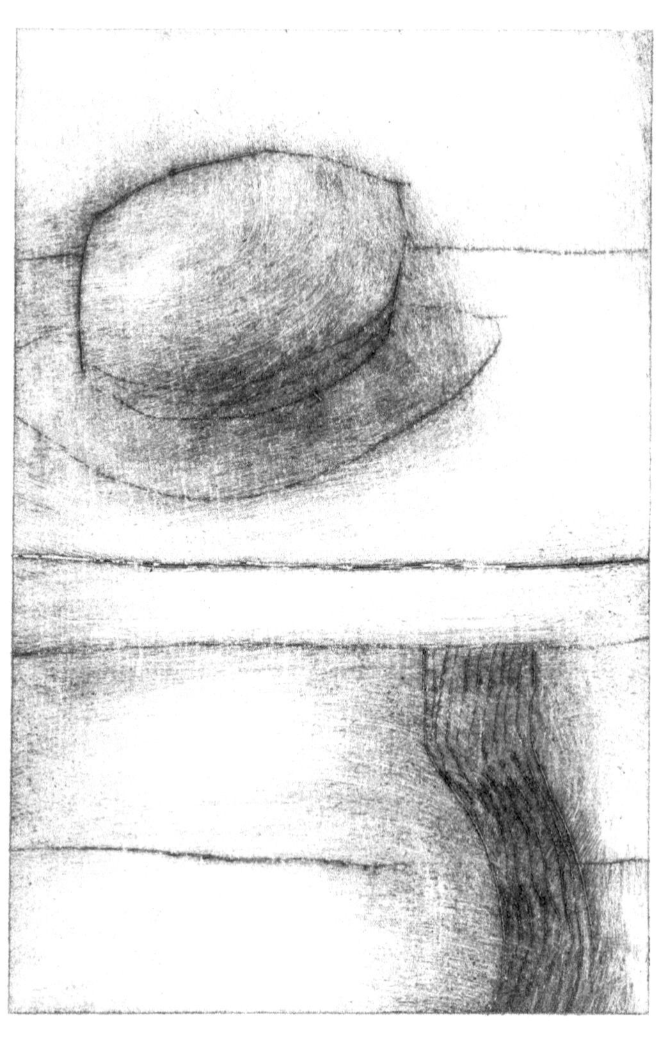

Walking Hat

NOVEMBER

1

Dream

A 'birth' through a very tight tube to a room with two people in it. How long are you here I say. This is it they say. I pull a long cutting – a plant – from inside my clothes.

2

No use taking the great view – need small view.

4

There is an active level beneath language through which objects communicate. Here and there the language is supple and fluid and special. Biffle baffle sniffle snaffle. The work or the life or nothing.

5

By doing by doing. Not what everyone else does but what you do, that frozen, that stuck.

6

Dog is my minder, boss, child. When no dog is around I spend more time looking at other creatures.

10

Starting to make new artworks for the exhibition at the Museum of Economic Botany. Using fine delicate Zerkall book paper and sanguine red shellac ink to paint herbs and then before it dries writing in blue ink right over and through the image so the colours flood together – finding the words while writing – like talking in a dream.

11

You can recycle biros, not birds, biros. Birds too I guess.

12
There is a symbolic African bird – Sankofa – which goes forward while looking back.

16
I have a close and constant companion with whom I am often impatient. He sleeps with his front paws together as if he is praying. His ears are like petals. His back paws are crossed. I pretend he gives me a compliment to butter me up and then I pretend I am cross though anyone can tell that I am really pleased. A small ritual. Aw Eno!

18
Really noticing the difference between morning and afternoon light. The idea of immersion and not knowing where you are going but finding it.

19
Six days lockdown. Hopefully only six though who knows. Eno the musician is always talking about tidying up his studio while listening and putting things together. We often listen to his album *Thursday Afternoon*.

20
Geoff Dyer – on rules for writing – *have regrets every day.*

21
Logic says no more large canvases – desire says otherwise – I have four in to be hemmed at the dry cleaner at Marryatville.

22
Herbs and words. Anecdotes/wisdom/silence.

23
This is where we begin. The technologies, the times we have lived through. The rhythm of words. Cadence. A painting is not a window but a door.

25
Losing the first fine careless rapture for second thoughts and plangent platitudes. I guess you just have to keep going.

27
Peach leaf wine, tapenade, cherries.

28
A snail on the path – slow/radiant/perfect.

30
The story of journals, notebooks.

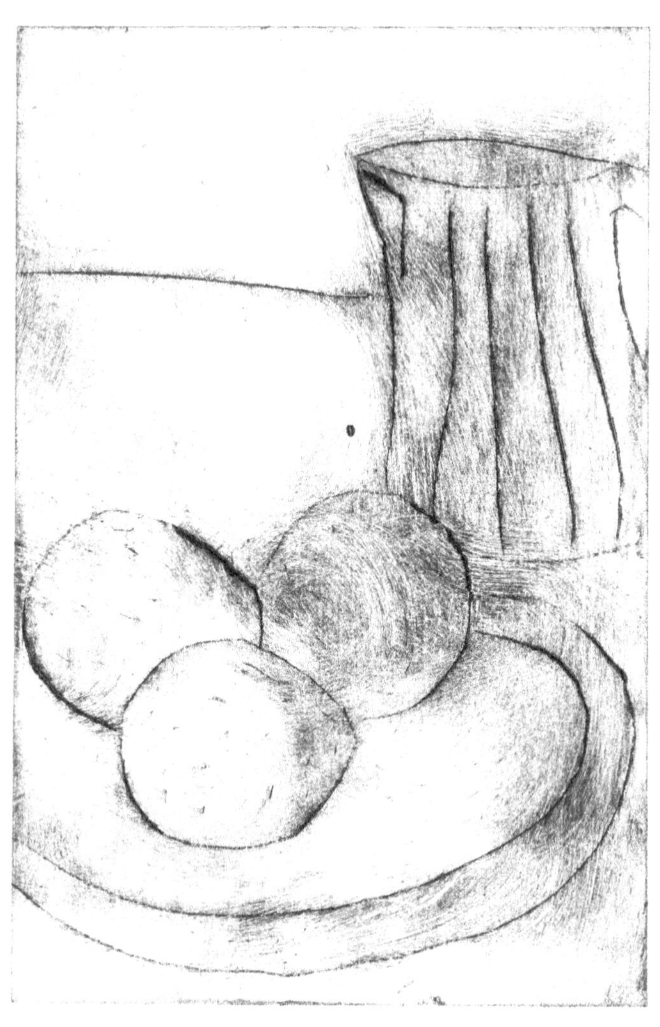

Still Life

DECEMBER

1

I like domesticity/grace/arrangement/style. I like walking by the sea, paddling.

2

In early handwritten books also known as incunabula there were nobreaksbetweenwords, non-naturalistic colours, words as objects.

Cool green silences in the morning garden remind me to breathe deeply, be calm and secretive.

3

The idea of a primer – learning to write.

Home Schooling is the title of my artwork from 2017 consisting of two large cast plaster books on which someone seems to be learning to write or brush or paint in a chalky blue. You see a struggle, a piece of time. Many children are being home schooled now because of Covid.

4

Yesterday morning in studio, in the afternoon some shopping. Eight works on paper – herbs and writing. Writing and image, layering thinking.

5

These new works on paper contain something like stream of consciousness writing. The texture and the colour of the sanguine ink stirs me inside. Being stirred what does that mean? Touched in the centre, the heart, the stomach. Every time I see a drawing on stone from ancient Egypt, that red reaches inside me. Iron oxide, red ochre, the earth, blood. Listening to thoughts.

6

Story written in bed in head last night with eyes closed – something about bookshelves.

7

That language can multiply itself and form secret and unusual patterns, while everything is put away in the drawer. Ania Walwicz

8

Realise I have a project. There is the journey and there is the story of the journey.

10

The plum tree is a bride.

And when I stand under its net, its veil, I am one too.

11

Nothing like illness to clear the head. Today empty I give myself the gift of nothing and ideas flow in as I sit on the sofa.

12

Eat like the animals. Which ones?

16

Song of Eno and S as pirates.

> *We are ne'er-do-wells*
> *Who have gone 'round the bend*
> *And are not coming back*

17

Stay calm be calm. Feel deracinated. My way of working burns things up. Sketches for wall paintings. Window works. A work from every window.

19

Lazy soft slow day. Will I begin today what I always plan to begin – an account of what I do and why? A catalogue of works.

Always I feel like getting going at the end of the year. Well usually. Making pickles and bitters. And writing.

20
I've been having a holiday, a vast idleness, indolence. It might go on forever.

21
An end to procrastination!!!

22
Gaps/gaps, cursory moments to work unselfconsciously.

23
Dessert for Xmas? Drawings for large paintings.

24
Cards and gifts. Dolmades. Nice cheese, goat and blue.

25
Writing as intimacy. Late picking. Gone to seed.

26
Seeing the value of intuition and the moment. Simplicity and not too much of anything.

Where are the pages of sages? Where is my folder of songs and words? Where are my words? The words I learn to sing and say off by heart. They are here somewhere.

Learn to listen/to respond/to be hardworking and not blame others if you aren't.

27
Inspiring interview on the radio with Mavis Staples, and one with a guy from Radiohead who speaks of – *when the songs started coming.*

28
The plan or the plot for the day – out/in. Plum sauce, plum jam, bowls of marvellous plums.

Once upon a time I read a short story in which a young couple painted their house in summer. I could never find it again but always remember it. Every summer I like to do some painting of the house and listen to the radio and enter that dream-space of stillness and hope.

The doorway of a poem/doors opening to meanings. Dog sounds – a light hum or rumble, a completely silent breathing. The fox knows many things, the hedgehog only one. I like to repeat this sentence over and over. A mantra or a koan maybe?

29
Seeing or focusing on deficits – a habit. Herbs and words – evergreen. A list of words on a scrap of paper, on a blackboard, on your skin.

30
Museum of useful botany. Leaves and memory. Museum of herbs – aromatic. The language of flowers. Insistent dialogue. Ways to remember. Words from memory. Words for memory. When you stop watching yourself, that is good.

31
The making of shade.

Inventory

2021

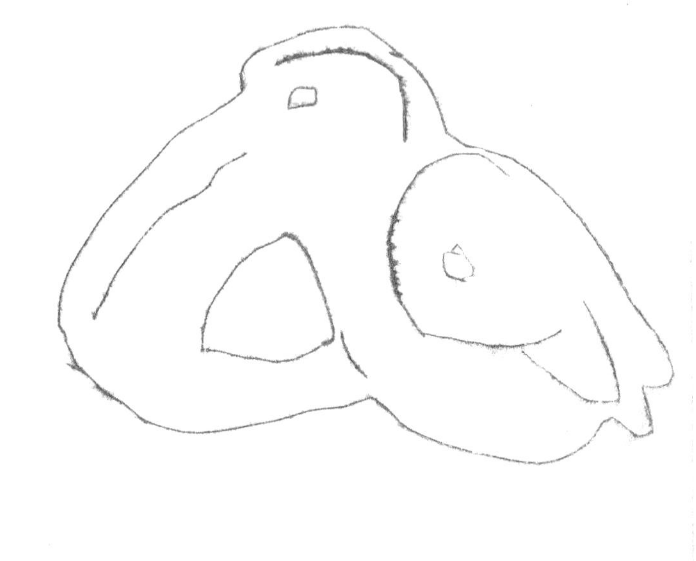

The world is a handkerchief.

JANUARY

2

The thing is to be absorbed in the work. To not succumb to despair and endless lying on the carpet. And in some of the work there is an incentive, a coiled energy.

3

I lie in bed like a lettuce leaf in a sandwich, limp and green, while the sun rises.

4

I think I have *amor vacui* not *horror vacui*.

A moral, a fable. Is Corona virus made in a lab? Thus being germ warfare.

5

Imagine having a tail. It might make lying on your back awkward. It could be pulled.

Your clothes would need a hole for it. You could wag it.

6

Arrange garden for eternity, to give love and compassion. What is a lifetime? There are no others. Always I was waiting to feel well. But this is it.

8

Eno has overdone it and needs rest. So no afternoon walk but a big bag of cumquats delivered to the local church donations table for marmalade makers. Might see a jar at the next election stall. Democracy marmalade, old books and knitted teddy bears.

9

On my mission to mend the world I begin with my room. I don't last long. I put a sheet of cardboard in the window to block the street light. Later a draught will make it shake and shudder and tap in the middle of the night. And wake us to hold our breath and listen.

10

Dinner for three – a big snapper with pickled lemon, fennel, rosemary, potato salad.

15

I touch up the missing black on the frames around the Japanese prints taken from books by my parents in the fifties. They are nearly as old as me. They are starting to break out in mottled brown marks. They hold time. They hold shape. They hold eternity. Because they have always been there.

18

Where *is* your heart?

21

The end of the day. We rest in darkness, craving solitude, lack of interruption, lack of interpretation, mental space, oblivion and so on.

22

One thought at a time, I become as simple as glass which is not so clear or simple. We are on the edge of the abyss always.

24

Brown and grey with tinges of purple. When you can see thought in a colour or a line then you are getting somewhere.

25

Every day it is the same. I push paper around. Will I ever make room for important things? What is a home truth? We are born to die, unseen unknown unloved, I tell Eno the dog. He is the only one who sort of listens, the only one who is here. What a relief he seems to say with his eyes and shoulders.

26

The Irishness of life – Biden.

28

I recall my etchings of hills and animals made in 2010 and shown at Greenaway Art Gallery. I wrote that the beasts, the beginnings of a contemporary bestiary, came out of notebooks and the night. There was *The Camel of Doom, The Worm of Death, Forebear* and *Dragon Tree. The Eagle of Ennui* is yet to be made, along with many others.

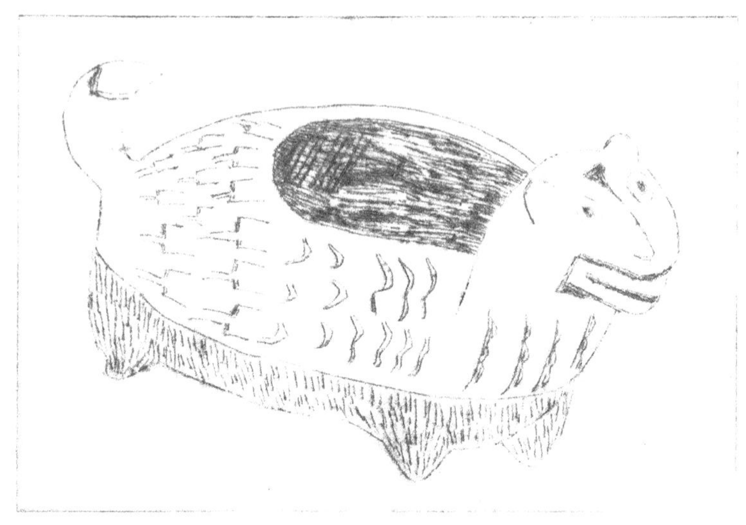

The devil knows more for being old than for being the devil.

FEBRUARY

1

Resilience and humour.

2

In storytelling there is a marvellous element of sharing and remembering. I love the way language slices through experience.

8

Bees making honey, collecting pollen from the rosemary, shaggy and waggy, their back legs have yellow beads of pollen on them, building up and shining.

14

To divide and order and sort my days and nights. Seeking the edge of things – where they start to dissolve, where they make your heart sing, where you see the light surrounding them, the space around them. Where the artwork seems to approach you for a talk.

16

Painting or drawing – how to describe the act in words/the feeling/the desire/the movement/the time after.

18

Sometimes we say a tree is self-sown. Rather than being chosen or planted it began itself.

20

Clouds are profound. Not because they think but because they are slow and mysterious and evanescent. Sometimes they remind me of nothing. A full nothing of vastness. Sometimes I see animals and adventures in them. The simplicity of air and water has a certain rhythm. A grand silence full of movement.

27

Maybe there is no right way to do, to be. I stand in the darkness with the trees. I have got into the habit of doing nothing, of being empty and enjoying it. The writing is to keep me company as is the drawing. It's a conversation.

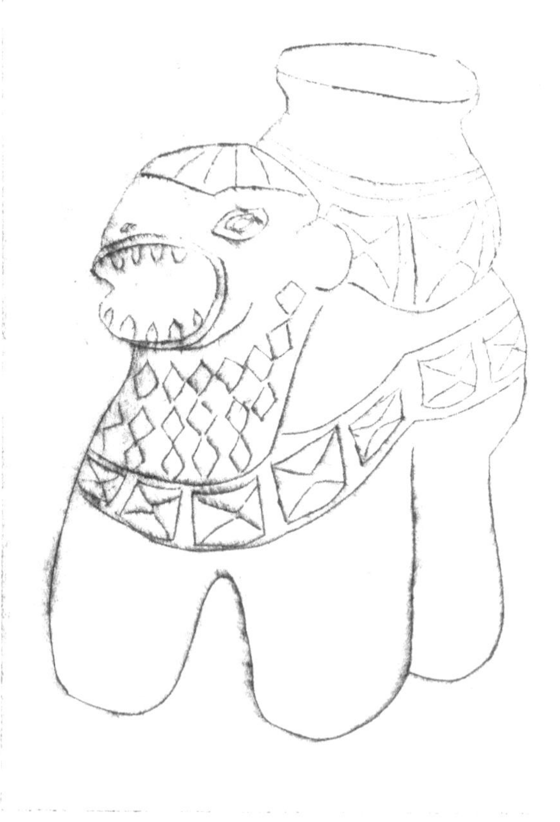

If you are given a horse don't check its teeth.

MARCH

1

I ask Eno what are we here for? Heavy question for 4 am he replies with a damp nose.

2

The scent of paper – vanilla, sweet/faint, full of memory.

3

A drawing contains in it the mood and attentiveness, the abandon and ease of the moment, which is to say all kinds of unconscious elements. I am not interested in taxonomy as a productive science but in the idea of it as listing and inventorying everything on earth, which really has no name at all.

4

What interests me in my bird etchings is the expressions of their faces and, as they are in pairs, their relationships to each other.

6

Your ears have birds in them like a totem pole.

7

Kill dog metaphorically. For being demanding and constant.

Forgive dog – try to. Does he forgive me? They always talk about unconditional love and dogs.

8

The body is a series of folds. I realised this lying with you. It is like a box of tissues though not shaped like one.

9

Alone in the bird loud morning the visionary hills, blue over red.

11

I don't believe in incommensurability.

12
The art of remembering is the art of thinking. William James

14
Writing is more than information, it is reverie, and memory is a book of pressed flowers and honey.

15
To bury yourself in the red and green garden, to sleep, to dream, to merge with your surroundings, to scent the earth, to be slow, to feel spaciousness/flight/song, to make something, to step off the page/the world/the planet.

17
Everybody learn to relax, goddammit.

19
Writing is like building a drystone wall, making something tangible with words that interlock and build up.

20
Launch of my book *Becoming a Bird: Untold Stories about Art* outdoors in the driveway at Wakefield Press. Kay Lawrence makes a speech with grace and humour.

21
Dream
Of sleeping beside my bed on the floor/Eno joins me/it's cold and I pull the covers down over us.

Another dream
In a shop Eno is there waiting for me/people are buying extra supplies/Covid is coming/I am trying to explain something to someone.

24
The library wants us to keep our books, not return them, and will even give us more – quietly passing them to us in the carpark in paper bags while wearing masks and gloves.

26
A casserole can cry too. Anything can cry. Pablo Picasso
(Transcribed in Picasso Museum, Paris, 2017.)

28
I want to begin at the beginning but there is no beginning.

To begin at the beginning is to imagine arranging everything around you to your satisfaction. To begin at the furthermost corner and work your way through the layers. Instead I often encounter procrastination, my deep need for secrecy and an overwhelming numbing responsibility for the past, much too much past.

29
I collect the snails from J's new house and bring them safely home to the garden – they travelled there by mistake in a red plant pot. There are at least a dozen of them, quietly moving, silently drifting in a brown paper bag on the front seat of the car, travelling back to their quiet refuge.

30
Could it be that each of us is born with a certain amount of patience and that we can use it up?

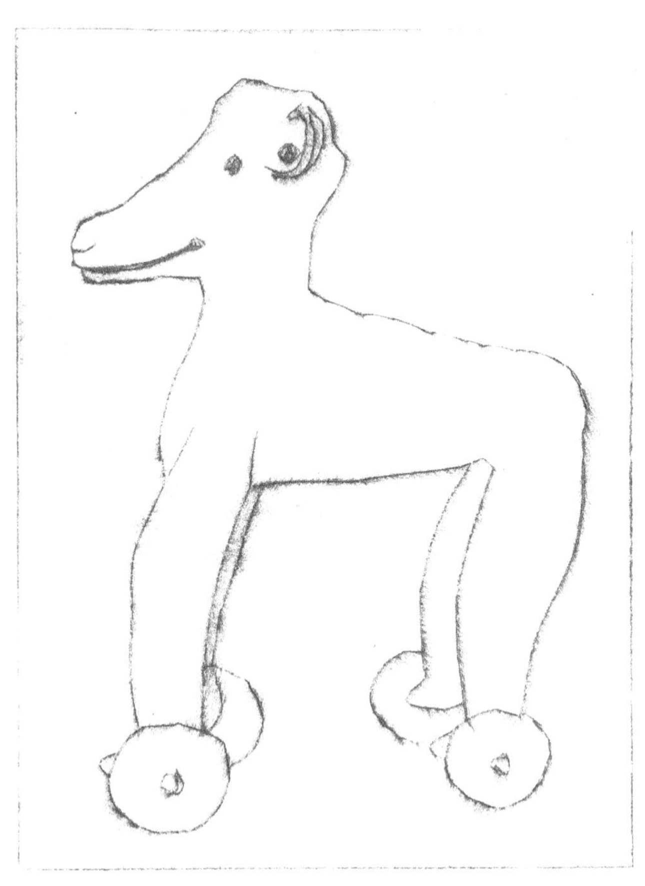

A good heart breaks bad fortune.

APRIL

4

Drawing limited by time – is alive. The rhythm is the thing.

5

He (the dog) is strong (too strong?) and the honeymoon is definitely over. Chicken necks at midnight!!!

6

What we see, what we don't see and the future. How we deceived ourselves.

7

It doesn't help to over-ponder.

8

It is not enough to stare up the steps we must step up the stairs.
Vaclav Havel

19

As an artist you are supposed to make things and sell them and sell yourself, which seems to be saying that to exchange things for $ is the most worthwhile thing to do. This can't be true.

10

In the absence of social life – food is the great discourse. I read in Eric Rolls' book *Sojourners* that the Chinese call food the first happiness.

11

Chaos with moments of intimacy, tiny worlds are everywhere. Every fragment is a home for some being. The geckoes and the spiders have territory. We must share the world.

12

To the sound of Eno snoring I am here again in the studio remembering. Around me I see charcoal drawings of the dog sleeping that capture some of his grace, intensity and familiarity.

Then there are the coastal profiles in sets of three on butcher's paper in loose watery burnt sienna and soft pink washes. To me they are full of longing and desire and suggestion. Then there are long pieces of hosho, the Japanese paper, blank and white, pinned up to flatten after being rolled up.

And six more pieces of hosho – on which gardens are painted in green and yellow and blue. They are full of light and movement and tranquillity. And space. Then there are two experimental frescoes of the sea and hills in yellow ochre, one of an odd tree shape and a monoprint of the sleeping dog in which he looks a bit like a sheep.

13

Somehow my mission or idea is to make an inventory of the world. This is slightly mad and slightly medieval not to mention impractical and encyclopaedic. And impossible. But the thing is not to think but do. Combining writing and images, overlaying them, asserting their equivalence, their translatability and un-translatability, does something for me, opens something, satisfies me like a drive in the country, like cheese, like honey. Or like children's books – always naming the world.

14

Each time I make something it seems to be necessary to reach a point of utter futility and give up then get on with it anyway.

16

We see an old bent-over man sitting on a bench under a tree. Eno insists on sniffing around him. I introduce him as the slowest dog in the world. Also stubborn and strong. The man says we have two whippets. He says very emotional, very emotional. He is shaky and can barely talk. I repeat very emotional and laugh. Later I think maybe he said we lost two whippets. O dear, why did I laugh?

18

Time to prune the fennel. Perhaps it will rain. The sky is half full of grey clouds. I wear my hat and a green scarf, cut the stems and collect the best umbrels of fennel seed – the biggest, best shaped, driest grey-brown ones. They will lie around the house to dry further on plates and then be stored in jars. A few very tall plants will be cut and moved inside to scent and decorate my bedroom.

There are enough seeds for lots of fennel tea and for chicken legs cooked with oranges and onions and garlic and potatoes.

Prometheus is supposed to have brought fire to earth for humans scooped out from the sun with/in a fennel stalk. The scent of the fennel is aniseed. Creation stories, origin stories, myths and legends – I remember repeatedly and hungrily as a child getting books at the library from different cultures and countries all over the world. All the many stories of beginnings and explanations and creations. I was fascinated by the variety of peoples … and their stories. Maybe that is why I don't believe in incommensurability.

19

I remember the piece I wrote for Hossein Valamanesh's exhibition at Sherman Galleries in 1999. It's the last two lines of each poem that come back to my thoughts most often.

Fingers of memory

listening in the silence
for rain
to burst
like stones on the roof
listening for magpies
awake also
and watching the sky for light
to echo the movement

and sing it
back and forth
across the sky
a creation song for morning
a song for the sun, for the day, and for being
everyday the same as the last
everyday the only one

The human finger touches sand and makes a dot. This mark is like a footprint or the tracks made by a bird or snake. It is like the mark that rain makes, both purposeful and random, it tracks thought the way a track traces movement. It is a first movement historically and individually, linking the present and the past. *I am here* it says and then straightaway *I was here*.

The human finger touches fogged glass and makes a mark, writes a word, draws a circle, joins two squares to make a cube.

Point, line, plane. These are elements of the creative credo of Paul Klee and Wassily Kandinsky and the approach to drawing taught at the Bauhaus, which is still used to teach the idea of three dimensions in Western systems of drawing. A point is one dimension, a line creates two dimensions while the plane introduces the idea of volume or the third dimension. This graphic magic is revealed to us as children through geometry and thus we learn a way of measuring the earth – geo (earth) metry (measure). We learn to draw a solid universe on paper, spiralling stairs, boxes in boxes, polygons and arcs, spheres and cones.

In Aboriginal painting from the Kimberley to the Western Desert, from Utopia to Arnhem Land, whether the marks are made on the body, on the ground, on bark, on board, on canvas or on paper, the dot or point is not about dimensions as it is in Euclidean geometry. The dimensions the dot touches on and its purposes are multivalent and polysemic. It can be rain, hail, sand, eggs, trees, stars … it can be more than one of these things, it can be all of them at the same time.

Pattern can disguise knowledge, clouding clarity and enmeshing information, which is already coded, into a matrix of dots to hide a too easy reading. Or it can be a way of inculcating power, lending the painted surface the brilliance of the plumage of a bird, the scales of a fish or lizard, the shimmer of water. Dotting and cross-hatching produce rhythmic structures which both contain and resolve complex tensions. As anthropologists Peter Sutton and Howard Morphy tell us in reference to North East Arnhem Land art: 'It is the quality of brilliance that is associated in Yolgnu art with ancestral power and with beauty. The brilliance, the Yolgnu say, makes the gut (the seat of the emotions) go happy.'

In his recent work Hossein Valamanesh is making objects for contemplation by responding to the patterns formed by plant life, patterns we see red on our eyelids when we are in the sun and close our eyes, patterns we see on our arms when it is warm and the skin becomes transparent, the veins visible. Forking, branching, dividing, meeting, joining, segmenting, all these organic forms he brings into measured and circumscribed rectangular spaces.

In Iran/Persia, Valamanesh's birthplace, the idea of paradise as an enclosed garden is imitated by carpets filled with stylised designs of birds and flowers, trees and water. For the artist the knots on the underside of a Persian carpet, as units making up a pattern, have an affinity with the dots of Aboriginal painting and, like them, combine function with meaning.

Valamanesh's works in this exhibition include gridded dots of black, red and yellow sands made in homage to the use of the dot by Western Desert artists, as the artist reflects on his brief stay in Papunya in 1974 when he observed the Aboriginal painters at work. When he asked if he could do a dot painting he was told: 'Yes, but tell your own story.'

Sometimes after I have been working in the garden
and I close my eyes at night to go to sleep
I still see what I saw when I was gardening
I see the mandala rosette forms
of green tap-rooted weeds
floating eidetic onto my closed eyes
Even if I have not been thrusting a pronged tool
into the soil to unroot and remove these plants
I still see a succession of them rising out of the darkness
toward me in a peaceful and beautiful way
Are they the ghosts of the plants that I have murdered
or have I released some image bank that is stirred
by proximity to soil and green things?
In these quiet moments
something has entered me
on the border
between the sky and the land
kneeling and touching
the horizon

22

Many sheep go by in a truck, the face of one sheep crushed against the side looks like the face of Jesus in a painting carrying the cross up the hill.

24

A flickering moment of clarity when Craig spoke about being alive. He is so close to death, facing his mortality with grace.

25

Many dreams about Eno, finding him, saving his life, looking for him.

28
J's birthday.
He is the same age now that I was when he was born.

29
Between me and the stars and the moon is nothing but time and space. We are all in the sky. And there's a dancing movement in the garden and I remember when I came back from Berlin after a long time away and spontaneously said what a beautiful place when I walked in the gate.

A dancing movement, up and down, back and forth, side to side, a dipping and a swinging, a sliding and a trembling. A shining presence of breath.

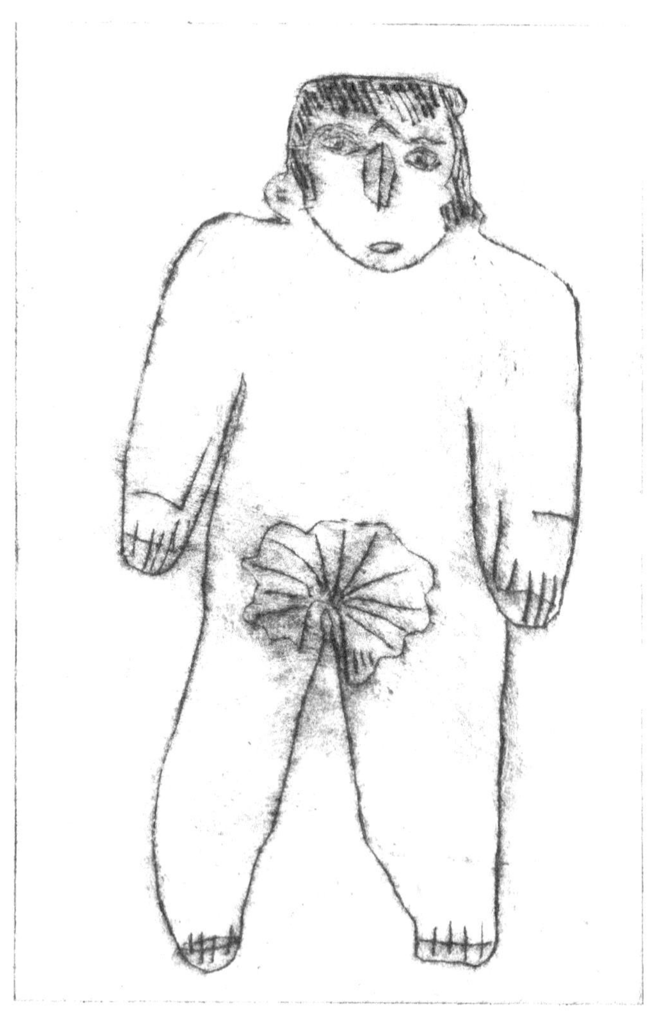

You cannot hide the sun with one hand.

MAY

2
Right now I could be lying on my stomach on the carpet with a cup of tea and a mandarin, a book, a notebook and a pen, propped on my elbows, finding words and ideas, making connections and rhythms.

3
Life is not only scary and nasty but messy and sad. Though love does exist. But is not smooth or calm or sweet necessarily. Damn.

5
The power of black – charcoal, ink, paint.

6
All the silences, all the silences.

7
Walking in a different place, refreshing my eyes and thoughts.

8
The technology is great except when it doesn't work.

9
J's take on lost things 101 – interesting. But what did he say?

10
Daniel Thomas said I was a poet.

11
Dream
Just before waking, sitting down to dinner and J was smiling.

12
I often find myself in a Bonnard interior. Such an interior is always an exterior as well as there is often a window or a doorway that he fills from edge to edge with colour.

13
From the library a Japanese book called *Tsurezuregusa* by Yoshida Kenkõ, a Buddhist monk, written between 1330 and 1332. Medieval literature. *Tsurezure* means tedious time spent in idleness. *Gusa* means grass or herbs, also a term used for a personal and informal essay.

Tsurezuregusa (translated as *Essays in Idleness* or *The Harvest of Leisure*) consists of bits and pieces – opinions, tales, musings, thoughts. It is said to be part of a literature of reclusion and hermitage and written in the style of *zuihitsu* (follow the brush) – i.e. follow the thought.

14
Dream
My shoes are each different – someone admires them.

15
To hide and be nothing.

16
Reading flashes of words not in a book. Stories like necklaces weaving threads together.

Memory, amnesia, ideas and poetry.

17
Read a great Shaun Tan interview – he says while drawing and painting the thing 'gets a soul'.

18
We aspired to each other to make our lives warm and friendly, inquisitive and alert. I would give you words, often funny ones, to show a wise generous and loving mind and heart.

20
'In the end I am as simple as cheese.'
'Cheese is not simple.'
'No.'

21
Mess, poverty, beauty. Eno up and wandering every three hours all night. Kindness, patience, gentleness, compassion, gratitude.

22
There are many good reasons to have books as friends. They are always there. They stay open after hours. They don't roll their eyes at your pyjama pants. They are steadfast, consistent and calm.

24
Life, said Samuel Butler, is like giving a concert on the violin while learning to play the instrument.

27
Words like sheep lying down around me in the grass.

28
Dream
A goat walking backwards.

30
I want to begin at the beginning. I like beginnings. But I also like to open books anywhere and read. Not follow the track set out but enter anywhere and find my own way. Reading backwards/sideways/and almost upside down.

31
We are the words, we are the music. Virginia Woolf

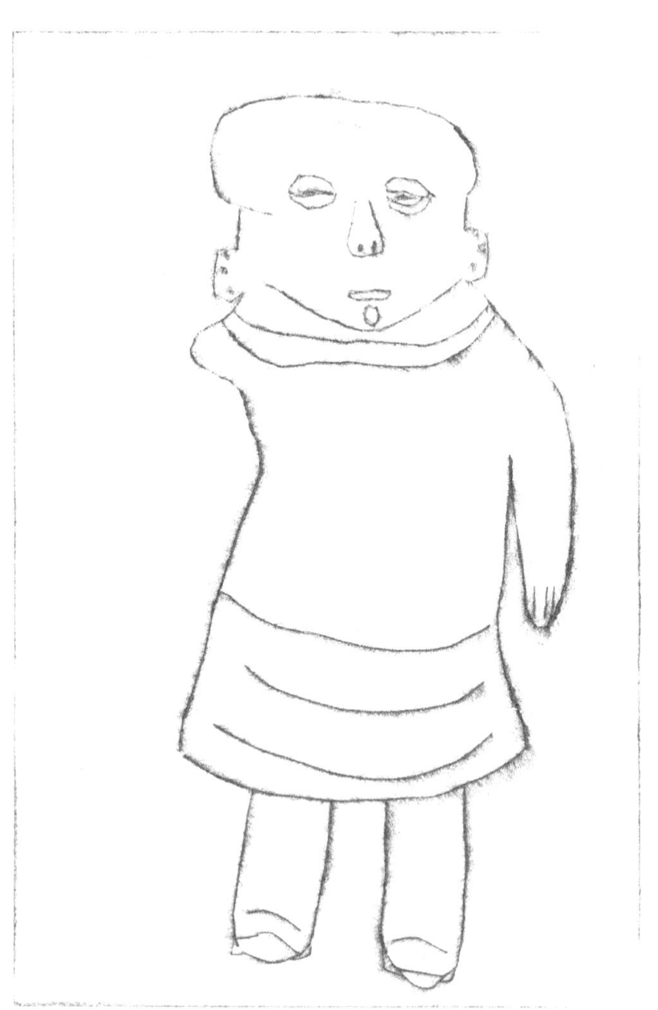

A melon and a woman are hard to know.

JUNE

1
Language is the skin on my thought. Arundhati Roy

2
Holding back, hesitating, procrastinating, making excuses, waiting for something, that clear space.

3
Cooking is not a mindless time filler. It is life/art/presence/season/delight in being alive.

4
Grilled red capsicum, red radicchio and balsamic.
Pork chops, mushrooms and wine.

5
For most of my life I have had a notebook as a companion. I wanted to be a poet but no one knows what that is really. The books are not diaries but records. There is no plot.

6
Once upon a time there was a little dog whose name was Eno. Only he wasn't really little. He was medium. Every morning and every afternoon he went for a walk with his companion.

8
Flowers from J for my birthday. Sunflowers, proteas, everlastings, ti-tree.

10
At choir in the back row we invent a new word wingling – a mix of whining and mingling.

13
It's June, what we call winter, and lots of trees have bare branches but if you look closely you see that, in spite of looking almost dead, there are buds of various sizes already slowly

starting to form and getting ready for spring. Grapevines are really good at looking dead and it is easy to see how they are a metaphor for resurrection – to be born again, to come back.

14

'I don't know why I am telling you this.' Said to me by the widow of a man who did research into eucalyptus oil. She tells me they filled his coffin with gum leaves.

15

I want to lie forever next to you forever in your warmth listening to your sleep. You make the dearest tiniest griffles of sleep like static only less predictable.

17

In media res – into the middle of things.

23

An hour in the print room at the Art Gallery of South Australia looking at *To the ice*, Bea Maddock's *Antarctic Diary*. She mentions Naples Yellow clouds.

25

This is our den. It's good having a den.

26

I tell Eno that you get smarter when you get older. He says then you must be very smart.

27

In the introduction to the Dorothy Hall book on herbal teas it says that the body doesn't lie. That is why you have to listen to it and its language which can be pain or discomfort or pleasure or humming softness.

Hall's book is a resource that I turn to again and again for its advice but also for its voice, what surrounds the advice, its tone and spirit. She is the grandmother, the aunt, the uncle, the old family friends I never had – giving me gentle advice on life as well as on herbs. Cheerful, humorous, resourceful, resilient.

28
Eno – trembly. I sang while drying him from the rain.

29
Wesley Enoch on the radio. Such a strong intelligent and lovely man – says he thinks he has ten energetic years left.

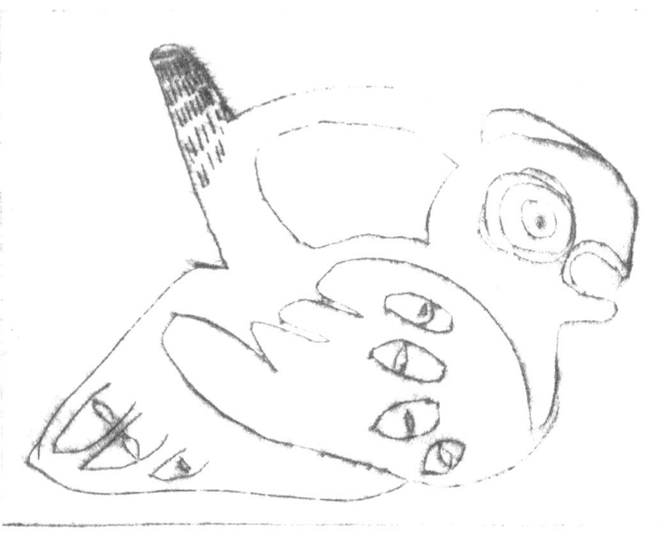

Who sows winds, reaps storms.

JULY

1

Every day is a history lesson. Every day is a story. The Museum of Economic Botany is full of them, tales of colonisation, trade, culture, ingenuity, tradition. My artworks for the exhibition *Medicinal Plant Tales* meditate on herbs and what they might be saying. Wisdom vs knowledge. Home remedies. Old wives tales. Unrecorded emotions.

2

Dream

An owl in the bathroom. There is another bigger one outside. It is a real thrill to see them, such solemn grace and bearing.

3

Fixing dining chairs with black paint and new brass screws. This feels so good to do, tightening the screws and painting the worn wood. Now to take them to get their seats reupholstered by the best upholsterers in the world who work on Magill Road.

4

The never-ending balance of dirt, dust, waste, debris, dreaming and working. Thinking about hoarding, and letting go. Doing what you want and need to do instead of rearranging the chairs on the deck of the *Titanic*. Or painting them.

5

I am not responsible for the history of art in Australia but it could be good if I was.

6

I spend too much time staring at boxes of paper. I gaze at old catalogues, notebooks, magazines and am desultory. My words, my life, are wrapped in them, and the words of others that I want to reread, review, reflect on. But must let go.

7
Citrus season shows up in boxes in front of houses. 'Free (the) Lemons' says a sign on one of them.

8
I want to know where everything is and know where nothing is. What to do? What to do? Looking at a Dr Dolittle book. He could talk to animals. The drawings are excellent. The words are considered. The animals seem both wise and self-possessed. Hugo Lofting drew and wrote the books in the beginning as letters to his children. The pelicans look so canny.

9
The air is full of green/grey mist, low light and rain coming. I rediscover medieval music online. Early music. *Hildegard von Bingen: Voice of the Blood* by Sequentia. Calming and sustaining.

10
There had been no house fifty years earlier; no farm thirty years before that. But the sense of the house and the farm and the people was that they had always been there. Don Watson, *The Bush*

11
Gardening – one of the things that keeps you alive.

12
Yet again the old restless feeling is bothering her. Margaret Preston

13
Words for morning, for mourning. Is all creation recreation?

14
Bastille Day

Vaccination/scared of unwellness, death (sudden or not).

15
Is Eno wise or just silent? Like the clouds.

16
I overhear a man walking past the front fence saying to his friend that he stretches in the morning for half an hour, then does housework for half an hour, and has free weekends.

18
Emerging from inertia.

19
Dream
I am in a poorly lit room with three people – all standing and I repeatedly say I'm free, I'm free.

20
Lockdown level 5. First AstraZeneca injection 3.30 pm. Watch out for side effects.

21
Words to find silence, to fill, to hold. Tomorrow to begin, to begin again.

22
Margaret Atwood on the importance of telling tales rather than stories. In an article in the *Guardian* about Isak Dinesen, Atwood says that tales have tellers and listeners within them more than stories do.

23
A fond memory. Putting a bottle of champagne in the freezer in late afternoon then going to work in the garden until you can't see in front of you, until the light is gone, then coming in and having a glass together, talking and making dinner. Another one is sitting, reading and talking until the room goes dark.

24
Out there in the night there are guardians, magpies who call to each other warbling across the suburbs. I think they do it for those sitting on nests to let them know they are not alone.

25
The most important thing – to think and not to think. What did T.S. Eliot write in the poem *Ash Wednesday*?

Teach us to care and not to care.

The stars are big and clear hanging in the night which is breathing after days and nights of rain. I feel an awkwardness around my heart.

The magpie – is there. How to write its sound?

Oodle twoodle
Dada twizzle
Twa da da da da da da
Dada daa da da da
Twas ooo da ooo twa

Air gathered around my heart, is it love or ghosts, or vaccination side effects?

Or my tendency to anger rather than resignation?

26
Today

Hospitality versus splendid isolation

Divine discontent versus Weltschmerz

Glorious solitude versus connection

The clearing out and the gathering in

27
So much rain in showers I need gum boots to garden. We must be in a rainbow because the sun is shining too. Hoping for sudden wonder and there are certainly moments of it.

Favourite books at present – for midnightness and to open anywhere, Derek Jarman's *Modern Nature*, Henry Miller's *Big Sur and the Oranges of Hieronymus Bosch*, Virginia Woolf's *A Moment's Liberty*.

28

Purpose – freshness not imitation and stay looking.

29

Grateful and touched by Eno's affection, his breathing, his warmth.

30

Starting to see patterns in my work – words and images layered, rawness, texture.

31

Move nectarine tree? No, says the tree.

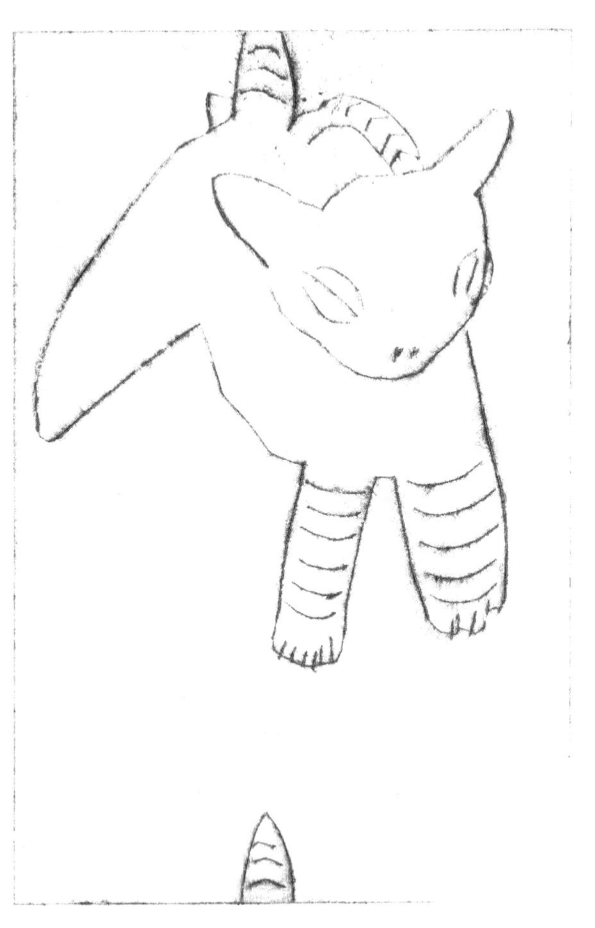

What does not start will not end.

AUGUST

3

Medicinal Plant Tales opens at the Museum of Economic Botany. Limited numbers because of Covid but there is music and I am allowed two friends. They respond in the best way to my work and he asks me where do the words come from.

4

Better chaos and love than order and loneliness. What about chaos and loneliness?

Hey that sounds familiar. Enough with the self-pity.

5

For some reason I remember those etchings of drawings I made in the Pre-Columbian Museum in Santiago in Chile in 2006. It was one of my best moments there, drawing in the museum. I titled them with Spanish proverbs I found – in homage to Goya.

6

I have no $, no resources, no hopes. I am the happiest man alive.
Henry Miller

7

To allow yourself to be yourself, to become a re-formed character.

8

The job at present is renewal and reflection.

9

Limited energy – where to put it?

> *I said to my soul, be still, and wait without hope*
> *For hope would be hope for the wrong thing; wait without love,*
> *For love would be love of the wrong thing; there is yet faith*
> *But the faith and the love and the hope are all in the waiting.*
> *Wait without thought, for you are not ready for thought:*

So the darkness shall be the light, and the stillness the dancing.
Whisper of running streams, and winter lightning.
The wild thyme unseen and the wild strawberry,
The laughter in the garden, echoed ecstasy
Not lost, but requiring, pointing to the agony
Of death and birth.

T.S. Eliot, *East Coker*

10

Languages of flowers/of plants/of science/of peoples

Language and plants/and flowers/and sciences/and people

11

Need to buy another cloth mask.

The vegan baron will not purge inherited furniture – a lovely quote from a great article in the *Guardian* re a rewilding in Ireland. I know what he means.

12

A feeling of grace and appropriateness/lightness and space/ *in hortus mundi/in the garden of the world*/freedom and ecstasy/ tenderness and secrecy/second-hand thoughts/postcards inside wardrobe doors/renewal and reinvention/living within your means, cosmopolitanism.

13

Life flows through us with billabongs and braided rivers and islands and a library – of leaves and bark and sticks and skeletons. And you can be reading and swimming in it all the time. Taking it in, moving and swirling, or stop and float.

14

There is enough for everyone and everyone has enough.
Deborah Cheetham

15
In a vast abandoned mouse nest inside a cupboard I find torn and nibbled old essays from my undergraduate past and find also that nothing has changed, I am still the innocent clutching the same somehow pure words and ideas that I always have. And it's there in my essays on what the poet does in spidery clear fountain pen, words on paper saying Quite Deep Things.

16
Mr Pinkel's pup was a hairy pup with round eyes and a black nose, he was hairy all over and very round, he liked to get up early in the morning and annoy Mrs Pinkel.

Where did that come from???

17
Eno lived in a garden with a lot of trees. He liked to watch the birds in the trees. And the possums, the moon and the stars. Sometimes he lay on his back in the grass and looked up at the sky and everything was upside-down, all the trees and all the flowers. Sometimes he would close his eyes and pretend he could fly and sometimes he would go to sleep.

18
Be ready to die, what do I need to do re the work. There is the prep/there is the sideways walk/there is the accidental and the real /there is overthinking and obsession.

19
I wish that I could lie in your arms but you only have legs.

You are a warm bolster breathing so quietly you stop time.

20
Dreams are fragments of ourselves that we carry in the day.

21
In a dream I open a drawer and find a mirror, old Art Deco with pieces missing, not broken but damaged, somehow it is me.

24
The darkness is for sleeping and for spinning stories out of shadows.

25
Dream
Dog goes missing after many other dogs have lain on top of him one at a time, not humping just contact/then they are all there and he is gone and I must cross a wide flat misty plain to get to the parklands. I try to decide whether to go back first for his collar and lead and think well I could look everyday till I find him.

26
Fables, parables, words, words, words healing, using words to build something palpable.

27
To draw a line in the sand, to proceed, to be always becoming.

29
Re secrets in artworks – it's there but if you don't know it's there you can't see it.

30
What has been stored up forever – maybe it is for a reason.

Two German words:

Sehnsucht – longing or literally seeking sight;

Nachlass – what is left behind – shoes, papers, photos, words.

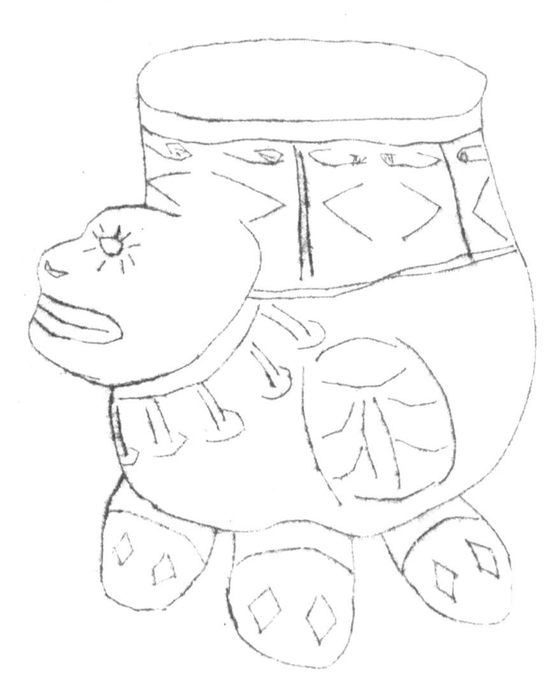

Don’t drown in a glass of water.

SEPTEMBER

1
The rain like straight hair.

Straight hair like rain.

3
Said to Eno by a smiling man – you're too old.

4
Four black cockatoos flying around as I park at the supermarket.

5
Dinner – rice with carrot and ginger salad, smoked fish and fresh tomato.

6
Life is confusing and full of the ill-conceived and untoward. Who is in charge here?

7
For you love was about self-sacrifice – why?

8
We exist in history, I suppose. We get up at five and go outside, it is dark and full of stars, magpies are sending phrases across the houses and up the hill we hear it picked up and thrown from bird to bird. The stars are silent white/blue on darkness. The garden is dark, the pencil pines point at the stars. Then I sing to help you go back to sleep. What songs do I sing? Often ones I learnt as a child. Christmas songs. William Blake's *Jerusalem.*

9
It's good being with you I say.

Its good being with you he says.

11
Dream
Mother and sister dressed up. I go to garden then come back to suggest going out but they are gone and two black dogs lie on the red sofa. Loyalty and duty? Love and devotion? In the kitchen is an immense pile of dishes.

12
Spring white plum blossom, palest pink apricot blossom with pink sepals, yellow senna, burnt pink crab apple blossom, yellow rue flowers, pink peach blossom, yellow nasturtiums, nectarine blossom …

13
To not know where you are going but to go. A sense of return in my work for the Museum of Economic Botany exhibition – a sense of grace and immediacy, of longing fulfilled, being not lost but found.

13
Dream
I am handed American dollars. Then I am driving in a car with someone enthusiastic.

14
The work is not telling you something but putting you somewhere.

19
Wherever you are you must create an island on which to stand. You want the gift of eternity. You open a new page and keep reading the old ones.

20
Illuminated books. Implied stories in the faces of birds and animals.

23
Days – scheduled days – unscheduled days. Everything, will, come, to, an, end.

24
Privacy/solitude/inhibition/mystery.

25
I miss two books (among many) sent to the op-shop. Both are by Jean-Paul Sartre, *Iron in the Soul* and *The Reprieve*. I think it is the covers that I long for not the texts. Though also the familiar yellow biscuit scent and feel of their pages and what they make me remember. Something about youth? The freshness of discovering existentialism in the late sixties and trying to work out what it was, a long word, a concept somehow resisting explanation but feeling subversive. Bad faith too, I remember that. It was easier to understand. The covers are Picasso paintings with lots of black. I miss the covers.

26
Season of dragonflies.

27
More dancing and singing.

28
Collect chairs. Red and black. Fantastic!

29
Rising to the occasion.

30
Pork burgers on brioche buns with apple and celery salad.

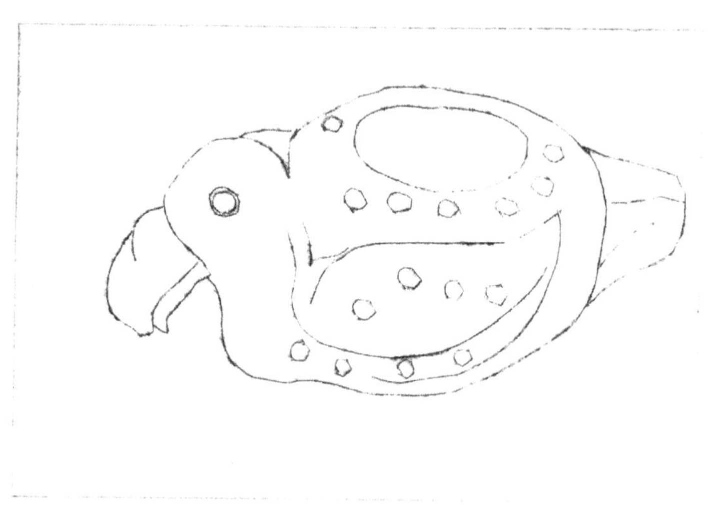

Love is like water that never dries.

OCTOBER

1
Do I want to be remembered or to remember myself?

2
There is art that involves technical brilliance, the still life, the orange peel you can scent, the shining cloth that you could touch, then there is art that stumbles but opens the heart.

5
I love the way the paint or ink makes the paper go stiff.

6
It's ringing and singing under the stars out there and big white whales are drifting overhead.

7
The snails speak.

Because we are slow. We are snails.

We snails, we are here to eat and sleep but what is she here for?

She thinks we are soft but we have sharp mouths and some of us have poisoned people. That zoonotic barrier, animals on one side, people on the other, we have crossed it.

The slow grey voices of the snails call to each other. They meet up and sleep together in quiet dark places side by side.

8
Dream
Woman in bed near sea looking at woman sitting on curb stretching and shining. Both are me.

11
The garden looks alive, says J. On reflection it's a secret garden. A place to disappear into the leaves and the hiding places behind them.

12
The writing as pleasure (to read).

13
In *Essays in Idleness* – there are words on white paper pasted on the walls of the hut as in my vivid dream in Alice Springs. A curious echo.

15
Shelves of selves. A series of prologues, repetitions, motifs.

16
This writing doesn't begin in despair. Well, sometimes it does.

17
My *Pages from a 21st Century Herbal* make me think of weeds, their sense of presence and endurance. The work is a collection of voices.

18
Everyday I have the opportunity to be patient.

20
Lucky colours in China – red, green, yellow.

22
Some degree of forgetfulness, fretfulness.

23
Is language abstract?

24
Making peach leaf wine.

26
New motto – Seize The Hug. There are a lot less around now because of Covid.

27

These artworks are like maps, old maps or the spaces between words on book pages. They assert flatness even as they suggest distance.

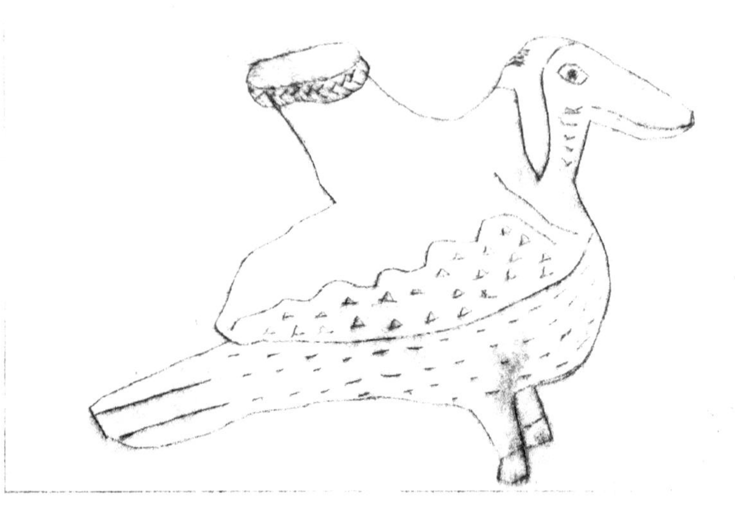

Each teacher has their method.

2

Dream

A gallery in a house where I destroy a few artworks. There is no front door says a large woman. Feeling cold I look for a cardigan and find my old thin grey one with brass buttons from when I was a teenager.

3

Turner left a bequest for 'decayed artists'.

4

Who would believe that the dog makes me stay in the studio by looking at me with his quiet brown eyes? I sneak out to do some gardening and he stands up from his bed and stands at the door until I submit and return. All emotion I suppose. Anyway, I do what I can in stolen moments.

5

'Baudelaire remarked that genius is the ability to summon childhood at will.' Quoted in *New York Review of Books* 4 October 2019 in an article by John Banville on Elizabeth Bowen, who looks/looked like a fairly stern drag queen.

6

The chain of the garden. One thing leads to another. The dark to the light. The shadow to the sun. The rocking silence of the branches flickering and fleckering the leaves back and forth up and down, waving and holding on, nodding and swaying. I remember as a child talking and thinking intently about the wind with such curiosity and wonder. The wind, the invisible wind. It travels the world. It can never be seen. Where and when does it rest? The chain of the garden makes a necklace for the sun.

12
The world is not made of cheese or bees or knees, well not all of it.

13
The garden is like a Bonnard – there are no gaps. We are somewhere and we are going somewhere else, remind me I am alive. Sometimes I remember, sometimes I feel like I have died, sometimes I remember to live. It seems to be necessary to find your way back to where things worked, when you knew what you were doing, in order to touch on the past, but not to live there.

14
I collect the music from the floor to put in my library. Some of it of course is ear-shaped, some is rectangular or round. I used to jump and catch it in the air looping and swooping but now with a basket I gather it from the ground to store and collect and hold.

16
This thing has happened to confront me, and all of us, with time and unfinished business.

17
In this silence I am looking for voices and find them on/in the pages of books.

19
The dog's soul is soft and warm and rhythmical.

21
My Covid activity to read all Shakespeare in the *Oxford Dictionary of Quotations* is a good one and bearing fruit. About Cleopatra.

Age cannot wither her, nor custom stale her infinite variety.

22

I wasted time, and now doth time waste me. Shakespeare, *Richard II.*

23

By the time you come to see me the person at the door will look over your shoulder and say she was here before the people who were here before us were here.

26

The afternoon begins at 2 pm when the sun hits the west side of the house and I have a cup of tea.

28

If you are a writer you always have homework says a comic book writer on the radio.

29

The air temperature is blood temperature. And it is very still. Perhaps we are in limbo.

Neither living nor dead but drowning in air.

30

Thou hast nor youth nor age,
But, as it were, an after-dinner's sleep,
Dreaming on both.

I always thought this was written by T.S. Eliot in his poem *Gerontion* but he was quoting Shakespeare from *Measure for Measure.*

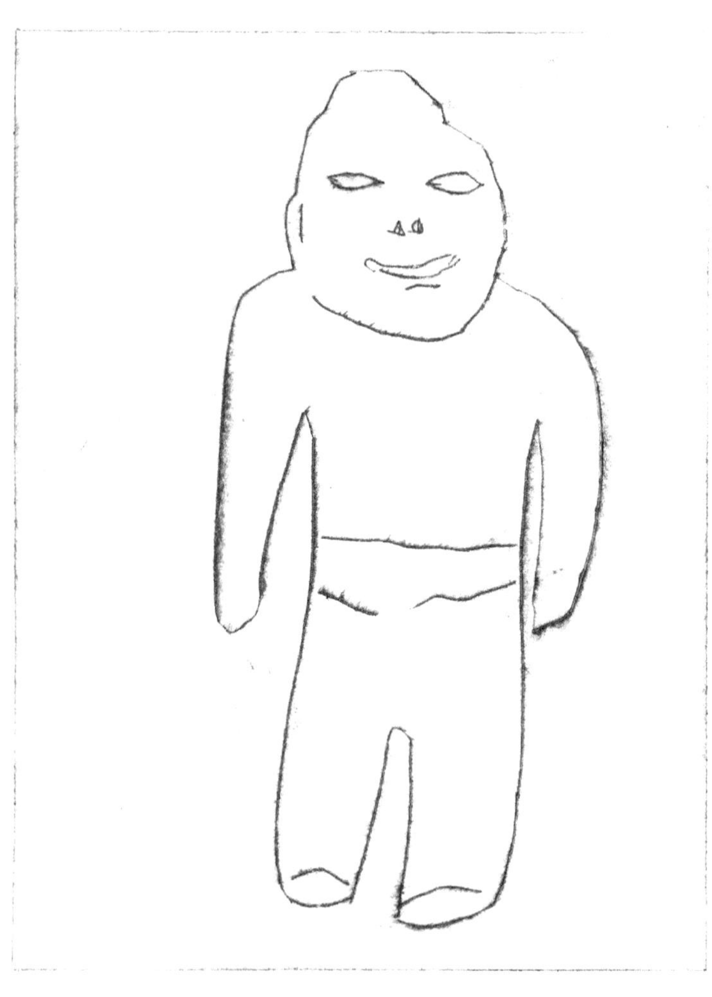

We all have a little in us of a musician, a poet and a lunatic.

DECEMBER

1

Let me stay with you be with you. I can be small and quiet and lie in the bottom of your pocket. You will hardly notice that I am there. My persona is cheerfulness, word play, funny noises, light-heartedness, the recounting and connecting of stories, events, phrases, places. The darkness I keep to myself, mostly.

3

Willem Dafoe makes a distinction between a craftsperson and an artist – the artist doesn't know where they are going. He played Van Gogh in the brilliant mesmerising film *At Eternity's Gate* directed by Julian Schnabel.

4

Ate toast with paté, pickles and misgivings.

5

Emptying out and gathering in. The soul comes in different forms – it can be a cup, a jug, bone china or earthenware. A bowl, green within or covered with flowers. A sheet of glass bevelled at the edges and supported by eagles. Sometimes it is a brown paper bag, thin and easily crumpled.

6

The weather seems malignant, surly, silent, inconsistent, brooding. We put up with it.

We live inside it also brooding, alternately sweating and shivering. Its stillness, the lack of breeze or wind suggests something sullen.

7

The greatest art is often more like a soliloquy.
Sebastian Smee

8
Looking at photos of my paternal grandparents Fritz and Gertrud when they were a young couple in 1913 in East Prussia.

10
There is no recipe for life, for living, is there? Courage, optimism, sense of humour. Dancing with words, prologues, epigraphs, codas. Music, song.

11
Halcyon days.

He follows me anywhere and everywhere, needing to sight me when he opens his eyes.

12
Small museums. Everyone to be allowed a small museum, a vitrine, or at least a shelf in a vitrine, to tell their story, to store their objects.

13
Purpose of literature – to make people cry or shiver, to be moved or shaken, to be made thoughtful, to bring tears to their eyes, to intensify longing, or create it in them, or make them remember it, to give them goosebumps and long corridors into memory, to awaken, to lull, to console.

14
Yes and no, but mostly no.

15
The weight of dust, domesticity and dreams. Dancing with words.

16
Awake for hours, thinking of everything, and notebooks.

18
On the immortality of writers – ancient Egyptian wisdom text – 'better is a book than a well-built house.'

20
I am a green pinecone on a sea of needles looking for an immaterial epithet. The dog sounds at the moment are quite varied. He is fast asleep and looks like an old mole. There is a hum like a train, a faint growling, and a rhythmical beat like a faraway owl.

22
All the birds in Bosch's Garden of Eden – red white black, swooping, parading, circling, looking, listening.

26
What we remember, what we don't remember.

What we almost remember.

What we remember that we don't remember.

What we wish to forget.

28
A slug in German is a *Naktschnecke* – a naked snail. When you say it, it sounds like a *Nachtschnecke* – night snail.

27
Ritual/routine/habit/practice/chore/ceremony/performance – what is the difference?

30
Some days my days, some days these days, my days feel numbered. You and I with our stiff hips, your four legs, my two stagger up the street into the light. Is it possible that we are no longer young, that our opinions don't matter, our lives are over, that our pleasures don't matter, are over, that we are about to become the past?

Inventory

2022

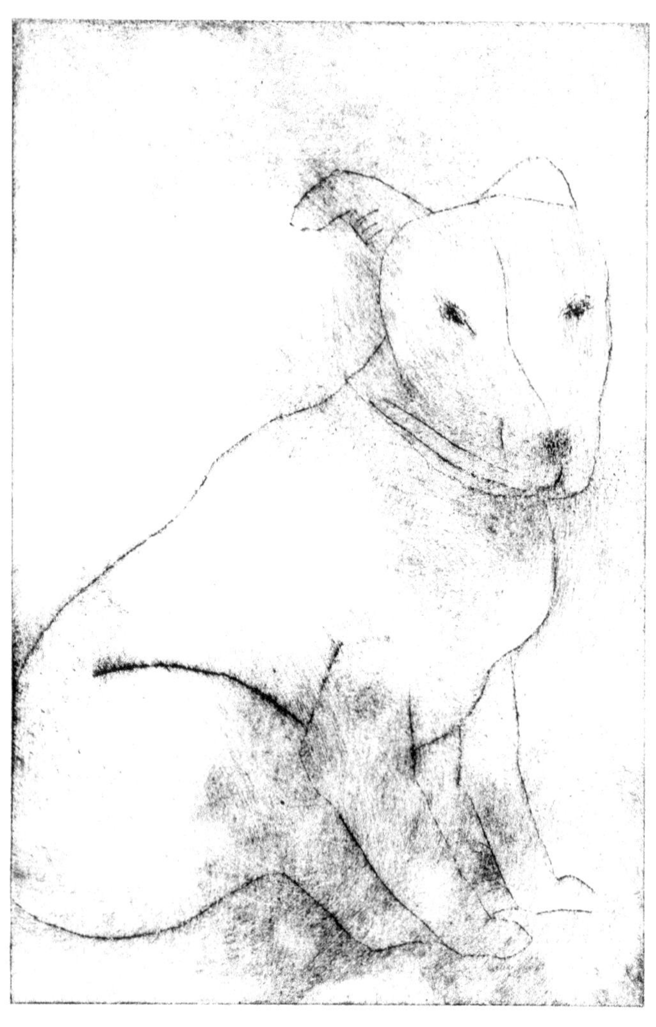

Looking In and Out

2

The black wing of death
dragged its feather over my arm
the black dog of death
pressed its body against mine
the black pig bristled
and the fragility of everything
made me gentle, kind and thoughtful
then life lifted its story

3

A very dark pointy-nosed possum on top of a box on the side of a gum tree, on the trunk above it a pattern of leaves cast by the rising sun. I see it from inside the house sitting on the green sofa and I get the telescope and it is staring right at me – we both get that feeling of being watched. So I stop looking for a while and when I look again the possum is looking across the oval and I see two small faces looking out from the circular window door of the box. Two rosellas turn up and sit on the jasmine then the callitris and the quince. The possum is like a sphinx with a very strong body curved over also now watching the rosellas in the cotoneaster. The possum doesn't know that there is another box in the next tree or maybe it does. I wish I could tell it to go there. It looks as if it wants to go back to bed in the box it is sitting on but then there is a loud noise and a big aggressive face shows up at the door to the box.

4

Try to remember why you are here.

5

The books I live with are turning biscuit brown or saffron yellow, falling apart or weakening at the seams, the joints, the edges. Though still strong, beautiful and … and elegant. The words stay strong and constant, mostly.

6

I rescue a child gecko from the saucepan of water near the tank. Then warm it on my hand for a while. It is cold but slowly comes back to life. It reminds me of when I picked up a monarch butterfly that seemed dead and the intense quiver that ran through it as it revived. Life as a quiver. I plunge the pot of Vietnamese mint into the water. I see a shield beetle poking its proboscis into a cumquat. Later I see a daddy-long-legs poking something into a cobweb-swathed shield beetle.

8

Life is not a story. Maria Tumarkin

9

Saw a magpie with a sore leg, a tiny bug with a big shadow and a spider looking in the window from the plum tree.

10

Buy three weeks' worth of essential supplies?!

11

Dream

Long black feather inside car. General good feeling.

13

Things there is no end to.

Things there is an end to.

14

Looking for a lost library book. *The Magician* – Colm Tóibín on Thomas Mann. It has to be somewhere. I remember throwing *Dead Europe* in the bin at an airport somewhere after finally finishing it. I am sure Christos Tsiolkas would find this acceptable. It is a disgusting book.

15

Today the artist Hossein Valamanesh died suddenly. He was 73. A gentle soul. A good life. Much achieved. Much loved. Gentle. Funny. Thoughtful. Gifted.

19

No doubt there is a belated quality to you, a reluctance to be.

20

What am I doing? Trying to review everything – all the drawers, all the cupboards, all the boxes, all the notebooks. Impossible task. Where is it going? Towards a clearer life, a cleaner death? Revelation, justice, understanding?

21

Making journeys into the unknown and known, thin places, fulfilling destiny, waking up the ghosts. Repeat repeat refrain refrain.

23

Talking it out with the dog. We know that love is work.

24

People publish collections. You have saved everything for so long. Are you writing/saying the same thing over and over?

25

We see a black Staffy with a silly gentle face. Dogs are for dancing, for joy and the moment, for smiles and clowning.

26

N and I speak lightly of life as the long death. Of the imitation of death.

The trauma of the excavation of the past must be balanced with delight and play in the present and celebration. Let sleeping dogs lie.

27
Words 'written' by the dog about me – is it doggerel?

She drank all the water
she drank all the tea
she will never know what she means to me.

28
Kenneth Rexroth on Tu Fu.

The poetry is the answer to the question what is the purpose of art: reverence for life, steadfastness, love, magnanimity, calm, compassion ...

Here we like to call it The Porpoise of Art.

29
Feel sometimes thrilled by my own work.

Then there is getting it out there.

30
Need to drink less, work more, play more.

31
Dream
The letterbox full of small wrapped Christmas presents.

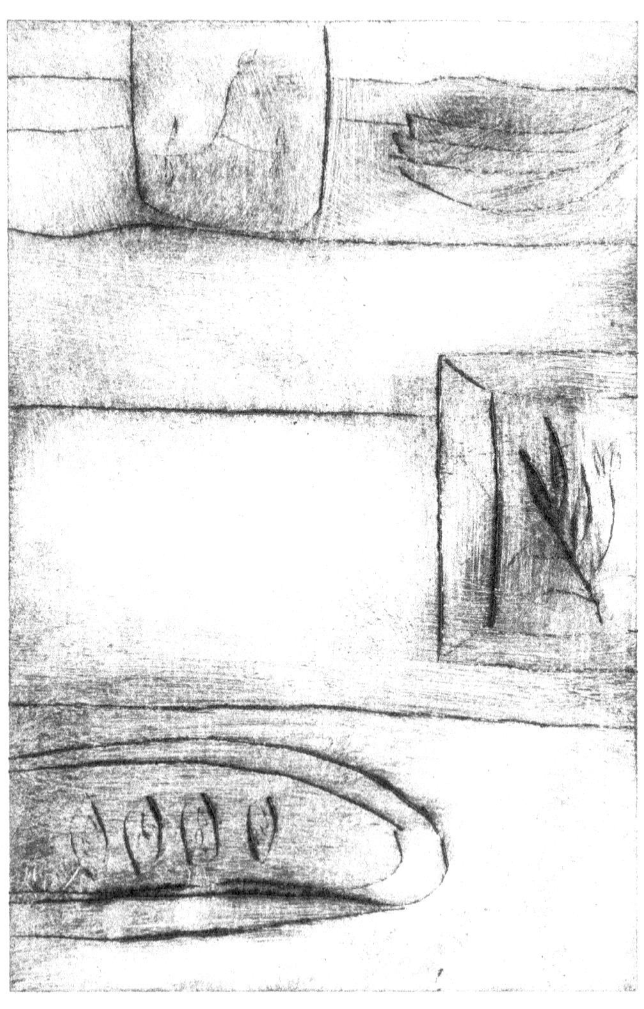

The Archaeology of Home

FEBRUARY

1
How do you love someone who lies around the house all day sleeping with legs outstretched and occasional foot twitching.

How do you love someone with closed eyes and piggy ears?

Let me count the ways …

3
The eyes of animals and language.

Translation.

The inventory.

The garden of the world.

4
Dream
My artwork is cast legs and people are enthusiastic to buy but renege. We sit on coats at the side in the dark and listen to speeches. Someone has made an artwork of a shelf with things on it – I suggest changes.

5
Housekeeping can consume a life though its rhythms can allow space for reflection.

6
Dinner for friends – steamed fish with lime leaves and tamarind sauce, stir-fried calamari and celery, rice, cucumber salad.

7
The two of us sleeping a lot. Our bodies flung down sprawling. You on the floor. Me on the bed mostly. Life is bitter.

8
Trying to get a sense of ambition going. Again. Stitching together words and moments.

9
We must be as clear as our natural reticence allows us to be.
Marianne Moore

10
Met with the curator and historian Lynette Zeitz at Urrbrae House re having an exhibition there. We pencil in August 2023. She mentions the light in the house and in the Waite Arboretum.

13
The dog is always ravenous, about to vomit and tries to knock over the bedside table like a steamroller. He sleeps a lot during the day then stalks the house at night, panting. I call it doing a Port Wakefield. When we drove there, 100 km from Adelaide, he stood up all the way.

14
Sometimes/often when we are in one moment we are anticipating another. A cool breeze in the still heat of night. The warmth of the sun in the morning. Darkness after light. Light after darkness.

Not only human but mortal, now I know that I am going I can let every colour mark my skin and the dragonfly sit on my knee.

15
Went to the event at the Art Gallery of South Australia for Hossein to celebrate his purposeful, highly productive and much rewarded life. His large retrospective exhibition in Paris ending on 19 February 2022 was called *Puisque tout passe* (This will also pass).

16
You grew into the garden or did the garden grow into you? It was not designed but breathed into being by clouds and cabbages and birds.

17
This morning while we are out on our infinitely long slow circuitous walk someone calls Eno a love-dog.

18
My father would have been 100 today.

20
The wordless languages of texture.

22
It is said that all writing is an effort to find that which has been lost.
Gabrielle Carey

23
Last night I wrote in the dark and described the beginning of the story of the notebooks.

26
I return to these words often.

> *A condition of complete simplicity*
> *(Costing not less than everything)*
> T.S. Eliot, *Four Quartets*

27
A boy riding to school gives us a wonderful smile and nod.

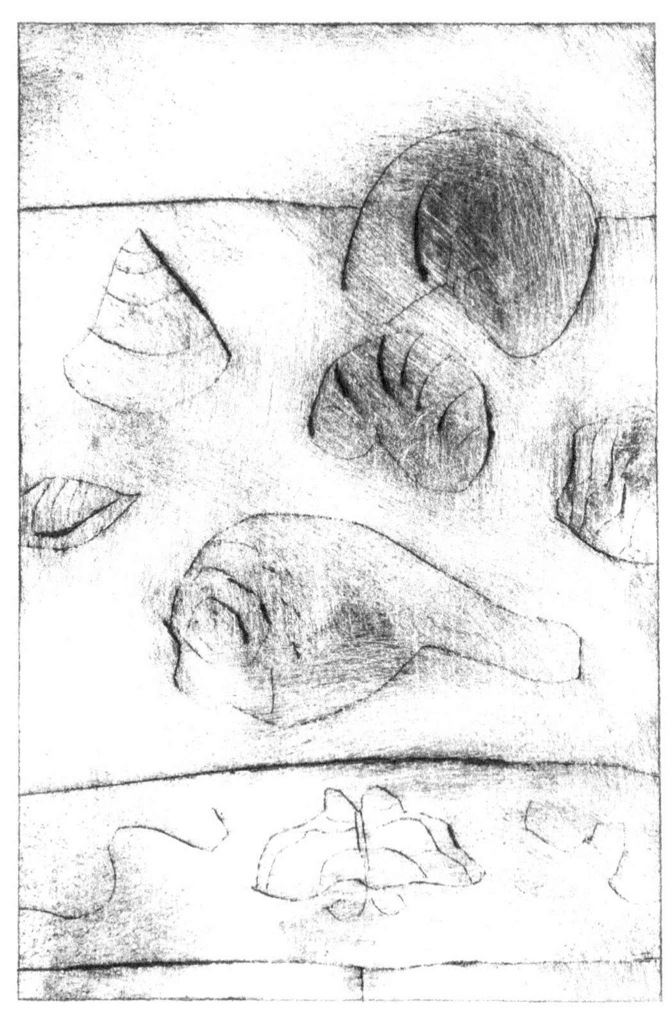

Shell Collection

MARCH

1
Drunk on words I live inside language.

2
Roast eggplant salad with capers.

4
The weather feels cruel. We should not take it personally.

7
Home again with deep gratitude, toast and blue cheese.

8
Cultural amnesia, cultural anaemia. Australian art: a vision, visions …

9
Learning to speak dog. *Mmm*, *nnn*, *uuu*, *rrr*.

10.

The observer, the actor, the dreamer. Tossing it off.

11
My ambition has shrunk to just sitting in bed with a cup of tea in the morning. It is one that I sometimes achieve. It has also expanded to encompass a vast record of everything and my thoughts on it. Well everyone knows that by now.

15
Some artists and writers have their thing and repeat it again and again, or seem to. Others have to rediscover it over and over, again and again.

16
We went to the sea for a marvellous magical day.

17

From a poem full of longing and memory by Peter Skrzynecki called *Red Cabbages.*

What was it about those red cabbages
that kept drawing me back?
I'd sit in the garden and talk to them
when I was growing up
as if I needed their company
or they needed mine.
...
Decades later I searched
suburban delicatessens
for brand names that suited
my taste –
not too vinegary, not too sweet –
until I found Kühne: Rotkohl
that claimed to be 'Nr 1 in Deutschland'.

Now when I eat them
I savour every mouthful
As if my life depended on it –
remembering those conversations we had
among rows of earth
and how they were never finished.

18

Trying not to descend into word spaghetti. Weather oppressive. Ukraine bad. Eno unwell.

19

Collected RAT tests. Rain blessed rain. The scent and sight of water. The haven of the Hahndorf Fruit and Vegetable Market – corn, Mallee honey, plums. Election – Labor wins, thank god.

20

Pull in your horns is a snail thing to say. For this snail human it means spend less money.

22

Painting trees makes me think of children's books. It's open, it's free. Large trees on thin paper, on canvas. They can be folded, rolled up like maps, are almost transparent, almost curtains, almost alive.

24

Dream

In France, flowers in my arms, leaving a party. Someone says can she ask me three questions. I walk and go into a café, I need to get something to eat. We sit and talk. Someone gives me a book, an old Penguin called *Women over 60*. I open it, the spine is broken. A sprig of a beautiful delightful yellow and red flower is in it and another on another page, it's fresh not dried. I touch it. It's wet, I say. People from the party come in, this is the place to be. I go to the counter and ask do you speak English, then can I order a gozleme?

25

Had to go and buy a new copy to replace the library book I lost. Eno whimpered when I got back. He never whimpers. Later on a walk he gave his creaking cries of longing on wanting to befriend a white cat called Leo. Mostly he is being grouchy, touchy and sad.

26

Elegiac, beguiling, lyrical. A calm small grey sea. Refuge.

27

Winging it. Undoing time. Rediscovering yourself. Prolific, profligate, prodigal.

28

I am making polar bear monoprints from my drawings of the wonderful photos of Dmitri Kokh taken with a camera mounted on a low noise drone on Kolyuchin Island in the Russian Antarctic. It was a weather station, is now deserted and occupied by curious polar bears. While drawing I feel a connection to the Inuit artists who make images of bears.

Entering the drawing I note the pleasure of it and the rhythm. The modulated line that flows, thickens and thins, curves and describes. Decisions, decisions, and being in the moment. Seeing and drawing the life, the energy, in the animal.

30

We're all monkeys here, apart, of course, from the elephants. Of course.

31

Drawing in the museum. Drawing the museum.

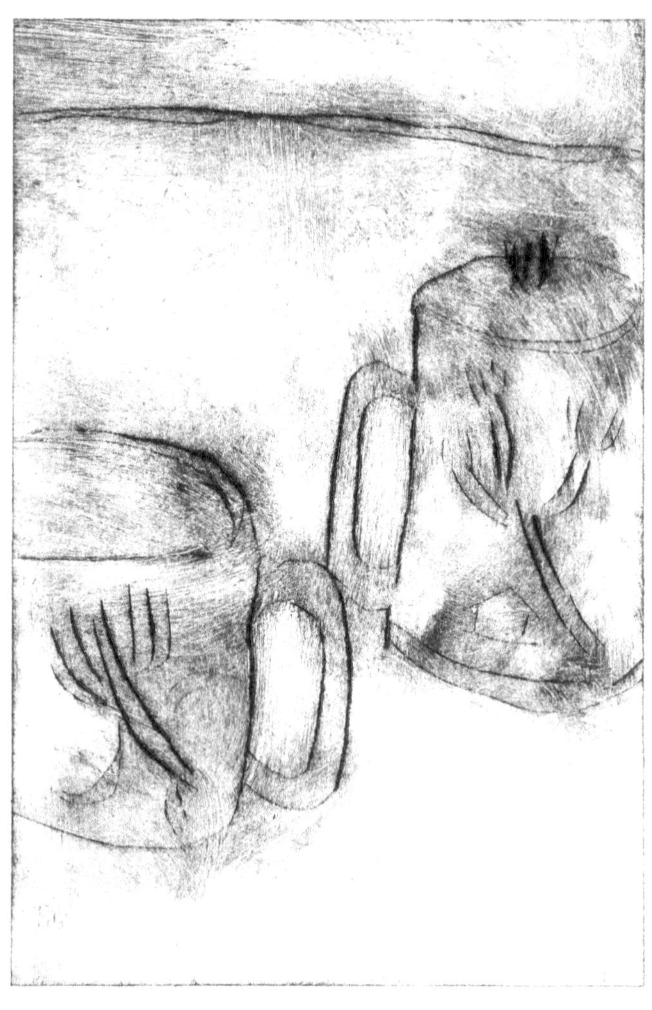

Tea House

APRIL

1

Words for Eno. He looks like a fat tiger and we have been looking for one for ages. He is just what we need. And by the way, there's an old monster here. He's standing on my leg.

2

In the Waite Arboretum as an explorer I walk from bench to bench, sign to sign, tree to tree. And recall the last chapter of *The Tree of Man* by Patrick White where, walking among trees, the boy decides he will write a poem holding both death and life. The last sentence of the book is 'So that, in the end, there was no end'.

3

The things we tell ourselves about how we feel. Do they come true? If we say we feel good, will we?

4

Overwhelmed and Underpaid.

5

Monostich – a one-line poem!

6

Parietal art. Parietal means wall. So wall art, cave art. They often call them paintings but mostly they are drawings. Most common – hand stencils and images of animals. The oldest ever were found in Sulawesi – three wild pigs – red ochre in a limestone cave. Warty pigs drawn with energy 45,500 years ago. Eno looks a bit like one of them.

7

I read a curious novel about the painting *Blue Poles* in which the painting is the narrator. And note some words from it.

She was at the age when women, some women, begin to live.
Angela O'Keefe, *Night Blue*

8
Travel – how strangeness makes space to think and feel.

9

You came in out of the night
And there were flowers in your hands,
Now you will come out of a confusion of people,
Out of a turmoil of speech about you.

I who have seen you amid the primal things
Was angry when they spoke your name
In ordinary places.
I would that the cool waves might flow over my mind,
And that the world should dry as a dead leaf,
Or as a dandelion seed-pod and be swept away,
So that I might find you again,
Alone.

Ezra Pound, *Francesca*

10
Four hours reading, six hours manual work – the schedule of some monks in a monastery somewhere. Sounds reasonable. Or maybe four hours reading, four writing, painting or drawing, two walking, two manual work, two being social, eight in bed sleeping, two eating and drinking and two dreaming, meditating, and staring into the trees and sky. Maybe there is a recipe for life.

18
Dog not well. I sing to him in the middle of the night. If you fall if you fall I will catch you, time after time.

20

Deep sea cod fish burgers, tabouli, rocket, capers, cucumber, rye bread.

22

Here I am on a soft chair in half sun with furry friend nearby who insists on my presence as a silent accompaniment to his sleep. If I move or go away for too long he gets up painfully and looks for me and somehow insists that I sit back on my chair in half sun near him so he has only to open one eye to see me. I am needed.

23

Eno catches a mouse at dusk near the compost bin against the wall, a young one. I get the torch. I am afraid it will bite him. He goes for it as a brave hunter, a professional ratter. I get the shovel.

24

Sometimes it was like a horrible fairy story. A sad one where a life had been spent telling the same story every night and it was all leading somewhere but never getting there.

Much broken sleep.

26

Must be that time of year when people reread old letters.

28

J's birthday. His garden is growing.

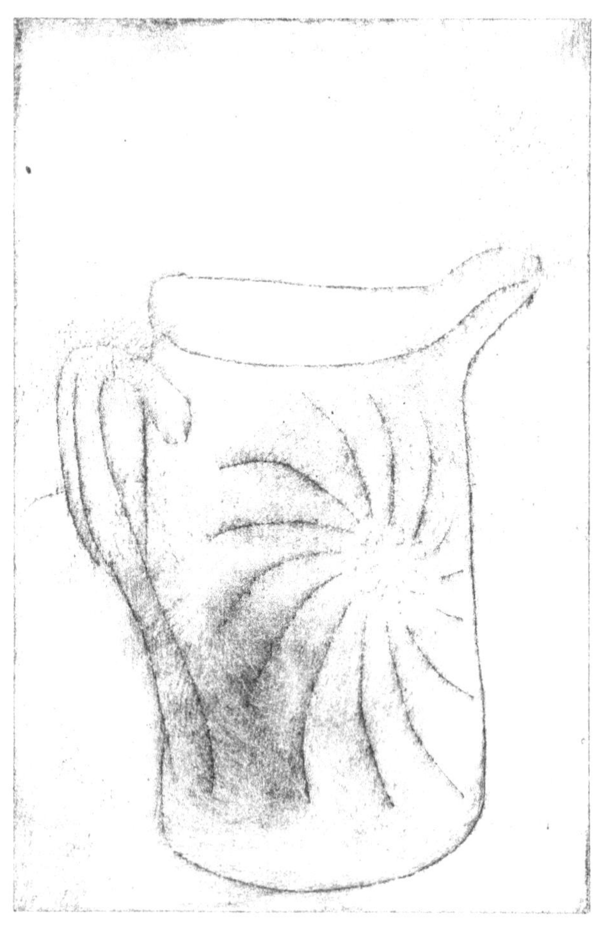

Jug

MAY

2
In an article on Chinese gardens on Wikipedia it describes how the 17th century Chinese painter Shitao wanted his work to create a sense of vertigo in the viewer, so the art affects the body. And somewhere else I read about first seeing the mountain in the painting and then seeing the painting in the mountain.

5
Fish curry – coconut milk, turmeric, chili, garlic, makrut leaves. Too good.

6
Covid – fourth shot.

9
Imagine a diary of dinners.

10
Whether writing or drawing you have to cast off into the work and that is how a sense of discovery enters it. An artist friend calls the artworks that she makes on the way to encountering the real work her stepchildren.

11
I read somewhere that an old dog teaches you lessons about patience, compassion and death. Tomorrow a dog physiotherapist is coming to see him!

13
Dream
A clothesline with my mother's things on it.

14
More walking in the Arboretum. Thinking about trees in art. Yggdrasil – world tree, tree of life. Tree stories. Language trees. Tree huggers. Tree planting.

15

We need patience in order to live. Julia Blackburn, *Thin Paths*

16

All I want to do is eat and sleep. And drink a bit.

17

Writing is devotion, explanation, conversation.

18

The creation of a personal library.

20

Life – a paddock full of weeds, or a paddock that needs weeding. Here it's not turtles but archives all the way down.

23

I heard the koala call my name.

24

Mortality, ambition, habits. Plainchant, plainsong. Mappa Mundi.

25

Urrbrae House's Arboretum Exhibition Room contains vitrines full of leaf specimens, open books and 45-million-year-old fossils found in South Australia just down the road from where I live. The Arboretum specialises in pears, oaks, dragon trees, banksias and eucalypts, and plants from places with climates like Adelaide – the Mediterranean, South Africa, Chile, California and the Canary Islands.

26

The other day after I spent time looking at some of my old artworks I felt like I had travelled somewhere. I was transported. I was moved.

27

When one is painting one does not think. Attributed to Raphael.

28
Don't want to try today just breathe.

29
Prepare to die – do the paperwork. Get your house in order. And live it up.

30
Great one hour walk with Eno – all the way past the giant Moreton Bay fig tree next to the creek. I must be calmer and kinder and softer.

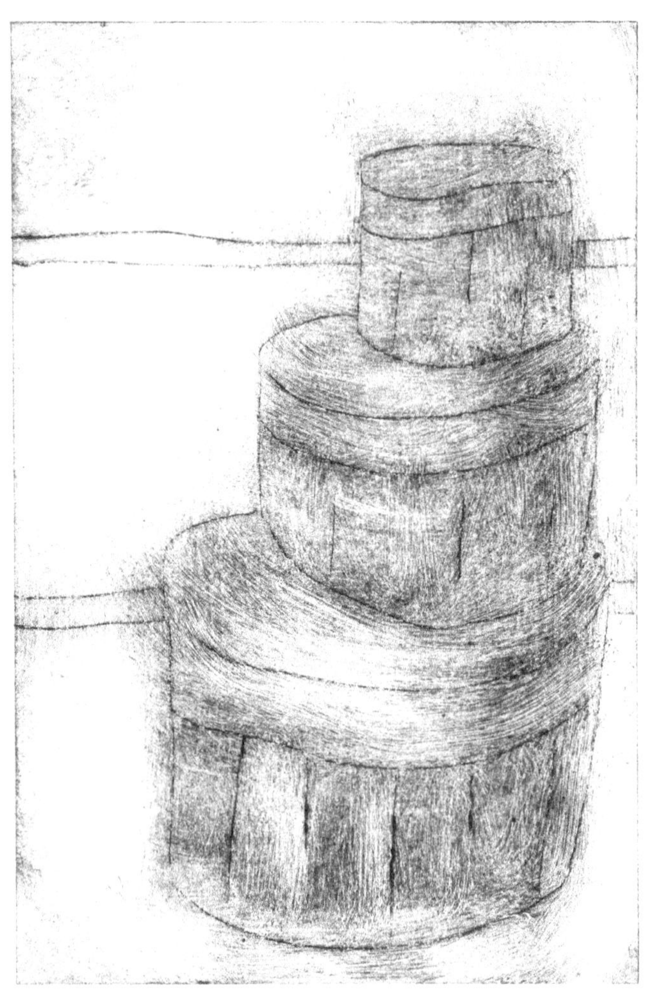

Sewing Baskets

JUNE

2
I have more unfinished projects than Leonardo da Vinci.

3
Poetry should be very brief, very clear and very fine. And trail clouds of the unsaid.

4
That inexplicable marvellous thing of not knowing how you made something.

5
Fragility and presence.

7
A week of going through immense piles of the *Adelaide Review*, to locate and save some of my almost thirty years of writing – exhibition reviews, book reviews. Cutting the pages out and putting them in folders for each year. Keeping some copies of the whole paper for the memorable front pages and their sense of an era. Bound copies of papers or scans in libraries are never as good as the papers themselves. Is print a dinosaur? But maybe one day we will need all this paper. Perhaps I should not throw away any of it or anything else ever again.

Lightly revisiting some days and moments. Remembering and laughing, rereading, seeing the writing – assertive, questioning, poetic, cheeky, alive.

8
My birthday – lunch at Brighton Esplanade Hotel and a walk on the jetty with J.

10

Director/curator/cleaner/gardener/philosopher/poet/kitchen hand/cook/shopper/donkey/artist/gourmet/connoisseur/aesthete/historian/carer

12

D.H. Lawrence's archive at Yale consists of six boxes and one art object. Somewhere else there must be more.

13

Devotion, indulgence, porridge.

14

Stir-fry chicken with tamarind sauce.

15

Evocative scents – bibliosmia, petrichor, geosmin – books, rain, the earth.

16

I walk in the backyard then return and on the edge of the path crush a snail. It was an accident – I didn't see it – I hate it when this happens – I must keep my eyes open. It makes me think how easily and suddenly anyone can die – from a clear sky.

17

Poverty poetry – the two words are almost identical. Is there a poetry line? Can you live below it?

18

Many erigeron are growing here, also called seaside daisies – a small white daisy-like flower with a round yellow centre, thin petals with pink edges. They remind me of my mother. They are easy to grow and very tough. I remember her saying as a toast – *May your joys be as deep as the ocean and your sorrows as light as the spray.* Very Irish. I haven't thought of that for years.

21
Up every two hours all night. Eno is uncomfortable. Vet suggests operation on teeth. What to do? What is best for him? Not to him but for him.

22
I sing Bob Marley's 'Redemption Song' again for Eno.

These songs of freedom.

23
On our last walk Eno mingled with the girl footy players. Still on the lead he drew me right through their small crowd and they patted his shiny back and *aw*-ed. The teacher raised her eyebrows but let us do it because he is so old. And cute. He snuffled through their legs and feet.

24
I feel bad that Eno is overweight. Port Wakefield. Up in the night, walking, eating, panting.

25
Dog knocked for six by tranquilising medicine. Stoic, loveable, spiky.

The kind vet who visits us says I need to think of myself. He has trained you well, she says.

I think you want your dog to be totally worn-out like old shoes or clothes before you say goodbye. He has a fabulous coat – soft, shiny, thick, lovely and always smells sweet.

26
Every now and then she put her foot down.

27
You can anthropomorphise trees and why not – they have lots of arms, are stable and good listeners. They are graceful and patient, elegant and thoughtful.

30

He used to jump on the bed, climb onto his armchair or the sofa, chase the ball and never bring it back, roll on his back and think or simply feel good being upside-down, chat and wag it. His most special and unique act was to walk excruciatingly slowly and delicately under branches of jasmine or fennel while they trailed over his fur, letting the sensations hypnotise him and whomever was watching – stopping time and going into an exquisite trance.

He used to jump in the car, sit in the front seat looking thoughtful, go out every afternoon somewhere different. He loved walking in school yards on Sundays finding bits of lunch. He chewed Paul's sofa cover, got on Sara's bed, ate Ruby's food, chased Madge up into the rafters. At Sandra's he curled up on an armchair covered with my jacket to keep him warm. He's your baby, she said.

He was often accused of being fat, ate lots of good things with relish, had his ears carefully cleaned with a tissue some nights, lay on the sofa a lot, met friends in the park, watched me cook dinner, was sung to when he couldn't sleep …

I had never slept next to a dog on my bed before but I have now. He was not in the bed but on top of it under his own rug. He kept a close eye on me. Had names like Wagstaff, Fuzzdick, Mr Pickles, Tickybear. One last adventure in the front garden – two crows, chicken neck bits and a black dog defending what is his. Today he died. Let go of life with a little help from the vet. He was really ready to go. And will never leave me.

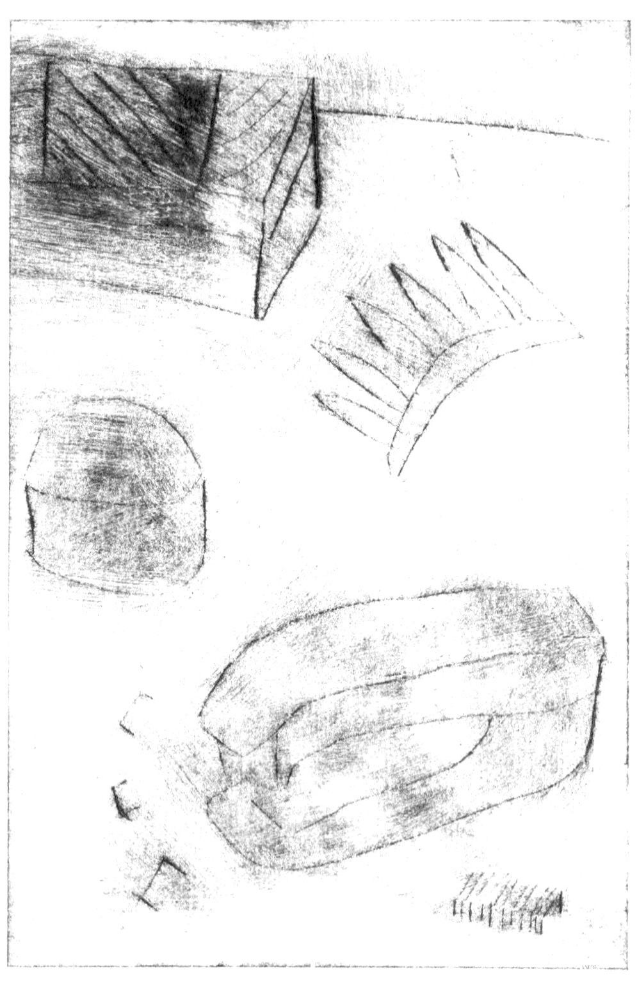

Deskwork

2

After what feels like a lifetime of stepping around sleeping dogs and those with open eyes drinking you in, of biting my tongue and going inside, the door is now open.

3

The brush is for saving things from chaos. Shitao

Quoted by John Berger in *The Shape of a Pocket*, which I bought second-hand in Berlin. One of Shitao's books was called *Sayings on Painting from Monk Bitter Gourd*. He stressed the importance of the single brushstroke.

5

In printing terminology a leaf is the name for a piece of paper. One side is called a page. A group of leaves is called a gathering. Eight leaves per gathering forms an octavo.

Shall we gather your leaves?

6

When you plant a grevillea you start a forest.

8

Made pastis with vodka and herbs.

9

The eastern side of the house always makes me think of Woody Guthrie as I was clearing the ivy round there one quiet summer day while listening to a radio program featuring his daughter. He left notebooks full of songs and she was told by the Woody Guthrie Foundation that she was the one to sort and publish them. She didn't want to but eventually was glad that she did. I have a CD called *Mermaid Avenue* of Billy Bragg and Wilco performing some of the songs for which they had to write the music.

10
After you died everything changed. My life which revolved around you and the devotion that I think of as love was gone. Time to start again somehow.

12
I wish on a star for ten years of being productive. Patching, gathering, riffing.

15
A bird is singing tremulously – ah a new poet.

16
Collected free RAT tests from the chemist.

18
The secret snail garden.

19
Health – rocketing to death, picking up a bit, or sliding to decrepitude.

20
Idea of fasting, of abstinence. Often everything has felt so provisional, accidental, hurried. Need to go calm, take your time.

22
Dinner for four – bolognaise pasta, salad, bread, cheese, olives, pear tart. Good.

25
The Waite Arboretum is more forest than museum. A pretty wild one. Full of birds and open from dawn till dusk. The Waite Institute campus, which is part of the University of Adelaide, has many departments and buildings and large grounds full of offices, laboratories and plants being grown for tests, and

scientists with their heads down, or eating lunch while staring at the sky.

Another great meeting with Lynette at Urrbrae House where I can hang artworks in the Drawing Room and also put some in two of the vitrines in the Exhibition Room. Both have large windows, pale yellow walls and high ceilings. The house was named Urrbrae from Urr – a town in Scotland, brae – a slope of hillside near a creek or river. I think of the many stories of diaspora from Scotland, and know that a bit of one is in me.

26

Dream
J comes to the studio door, smiling, smiling.

27

Rice, squid, chili sauce.

28

Behind the person being interviewed about Myanmar is a picture on the wall – I thought it was a green cloud loosely hanging in an orange sky but it turned out to be a man in army uniform. If I was the interviewer I would have asked about it. I do hope for justice for the brave people of Myanmar.

30

I have to become less insular, more peninsular.

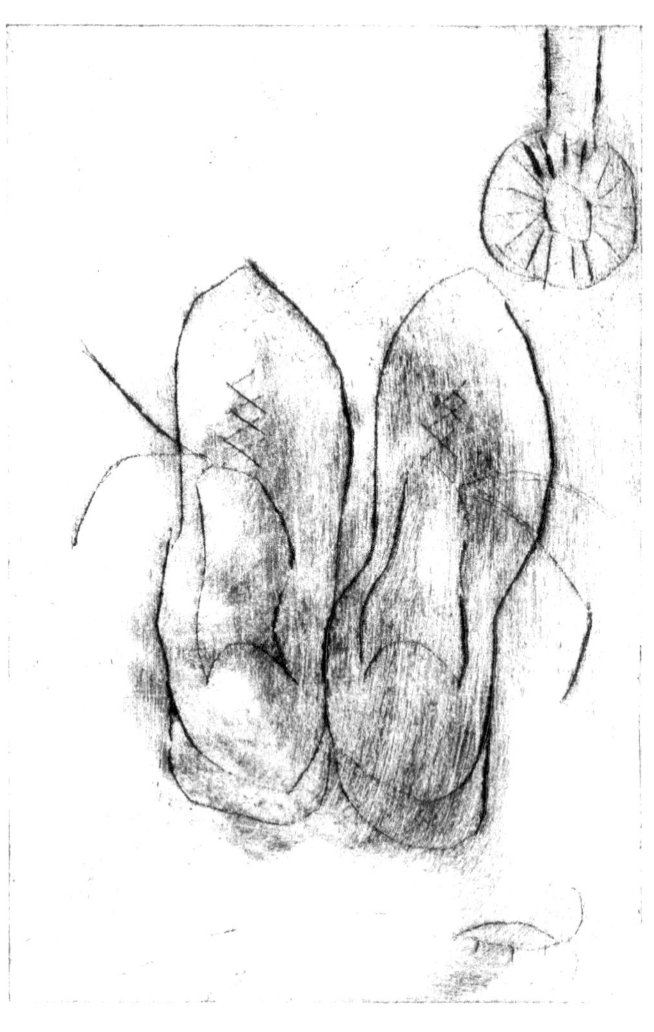

Running Shoes

AUGUST

2
The nursery tree is the native frangipani in which three young magpies still fluffy in their bodies sit. They are making I'm hungry noises. I think they might want to stay babies and be looked after forever.

3
Relict scrub, remnant.

5
Animals with clear cheerful eyes.

6
Now I know how important it is for me to stay wild and not try to be clever or overthink. Better to spill and flow and find the reverie unconsciously. It is like entering a forest and being a tree, one among many, many among one.

7
A gathering in the Drawing Room. A sea of tea. A sea of trees. The habit of giving.

8
Raingardens – a book allowed to touch another.

10
On thinking about why I write I remembered that amnesia is a driving force.

11
To draw a line/a horizontal line that divides the past from the future, that starts to line things up.

12
Trying to do systematically what can't be done that way.

13
Artefacts/shards/fragments. Coasters, cardboard and calendars.

14
Imagine walking back in time. That is what old notebooks do. Time travel.

16
Yesterday my research led to Ludwig Leichardt, Voss and Patrick White because of the fabulous *Araucaria bidwillii*, the bunya bunya pine.

18
In this dawning morning that starts at 2 am I stutter around the day and its words. I can't cure or mend either you or me.

19
In the drawing the dog's eyes look in and out at the same time. In one drawing he is thinking about you, in another he is clearly pretending that you are not there. How is this done? I don't know.

20
I think about how things outside you affect what is within. Objects of desire – not expensive but chosen, inherited, treasured. A shoe, a scarf, a candle, a cloth, a bowl. Scent, colour and texture that speak.

21
This evening twilight is like dawn – the clear bright luminous fade from colour to colour pink yellow blue only to the west – can the sun really be going and not coming? A bit later there is a star in the blue-grey sky and then there are the Pointers one by one and then most of the Southern Cross.

I recall once saying to my mother why do they have to bring religion into everything and she said, No it's a cross, not that cross. Eno and I often noted the position of the Cross above the house. And I recited the title of the book by D'Arcy Niland – *Call Me When the Cross Turns Over.*

22
The notebooks are a garden too, rather old, rather overgrown, rather wild.

23
Mushroom omelette with chicory. Salmon with fennel.

25
The things you like don't have to have meaning or purpose.

28
A notebook opens on an exhortation from Katherine Mansfield about risk.

29
A tree stays in one place. A tree reaches for the sky. The apple doesn't fall far from the tree. The writing is like a raft on which there are animals floating. Does that make it an ark?

31
Don't complain, don't kvetch. Don't whine, don't explain.

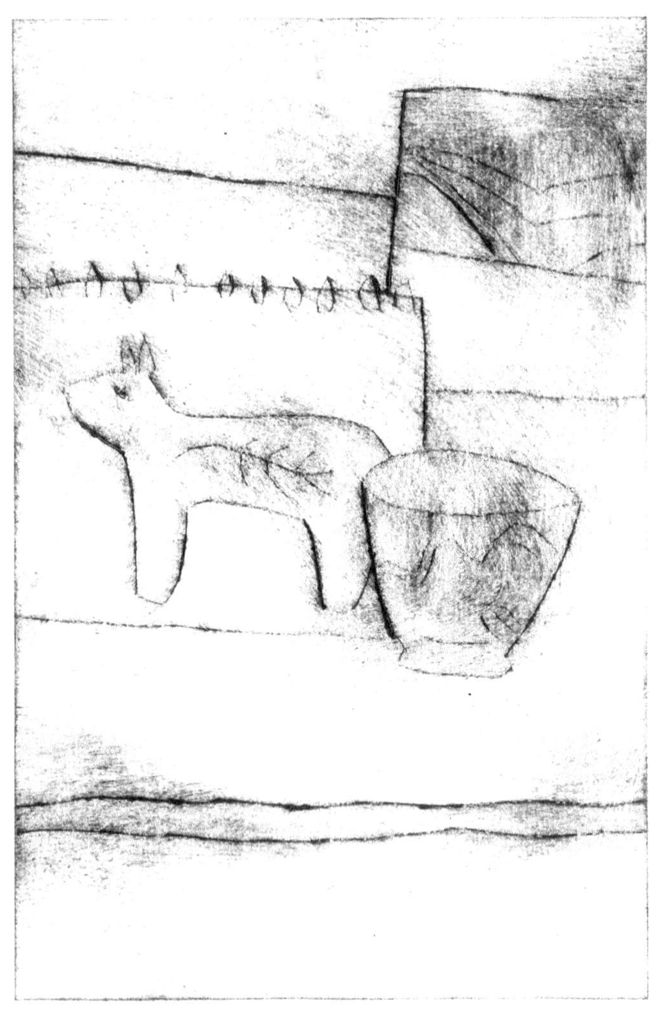

A Moment in Time

SEPTEMBER

1

Dream

I walk through a crowded street, study faces, go in a café, have to go upstairs to meet someone. In the corner there is a ladder to climb but it's hard to get off it. Finally I walk out onto a large roof garden where groups of friendly people in fancy outfits are dancing.

2

Heard George Miller on the radio talking about storytelling to make sense of chaos.

4

Transcribing the last chapter of *The Tree of Man* with red ink and brush on exquisite Zerkall book paper for an illuminated book to show at the exhibition. I will paint trees in green on each page on top of the writing. When the ink dries the words will still be legible. The paper is fine and delicate and the end of an era as the Zerkall Paper Factory in Germany was badly affected by the 2021 summer floods and will no longer make paper.

5

Happy-mad or sad-mad? Hiding and freedom.

7

In the world but not of the world.

8

My magpie child Snowy is warbling in the rain on his tree – such a brave bird. As he is young he has lots of white feathers on his head.

9

Paintings – transparency and opacity – emotional layers. Red/ purple over green, purple/red washy under green, red and green, red on white, yellow over green, watery green over yellow, pink over green, pink and green side by side.

10

Memory of being in the garden with Eno at night, all black and silver and white, beads of water hanging on everything.

11

Am I planting a forest in the garden? Well yes actually.

12

Words can slow the looking.

19

From the library I borrow *Book of Lists* and find in it a few shopping lists made by Michelangelo in 1518. They are handwritten in brown ink, words next to little images. I copy them out and their translations. Bread rolls, salad, spinach, fennel, herring, anchovies, tortelli, jugs of wine, dry or full-bodied.

18

Egyptians located the soul in the heart. Descartes thought it was in the gall bladder. Virginia Woolf *knew* it was in the spine.

19

Shelfishness. Much of that here. Arrangements and leaning books, and objects telling stories and shaping space.

20

The great revelation perhaps never did come.
Virginia Woolf, *To the Lighthouse*

21

Undone things. Too many to count.

Things that could be better. Things that are good enough.

To not be constantly arranging and yet to arrange.

To not be constantly sorting and yet to sort.

To not be constantly thinking and yet to think.

22

Who remembers the riddle why is the cook cruel? Because she beats the eggs and whips the cream. I could never understand this as a child. Why? Why? I would ask.

Today as I cut the eyes from a potato I remembered it. It is tied to cooking and the kitchen – the activities, words and objects used there. I can't help thinking of potatoes as gentle and reliable. I love them. And I cut them up. J tells me there is a Marge Simpson meme about potatoes. Marge says that they are neat.

Kitchen lore appeals to me hugely. Back in the sixties I found an old yellowing copy of the Country Women's Association cookbook belonging to my maternal grandmother Gladys, or maybe her mother who looked after my mother while Gladys was working or living elsewhere and who was more of a cook. And was said to have a light hand with scones. Or was that Aunty Dorrie?

We never spent much time with Gladys. She lived in Melbourne and we were in America, Austria or Adelaide, though she did visit us in the US and saw me take my first steps in Golden Gate Park in San Francisco. And she helped my mother during my first year in the bush at Ringwood in Victoria.

Uncannily after thinking about her I went through a drawer of postcards and found one from her that I cannot remember ever seeing before. It's to me from Scotland and she signed it Nanbo.

As a teenager I cooked my way through the cake and biscuit section of the CWA cookbook. Maybe the idea of being a countrywoman appealed to me. One night I destroyed the old Mixmaster, horrible smelly smoke came pouring out of it. My mother bought me a new one, which I still use, it is vintage now. Its brown base has that almost organic aura of old plastic.

I especially enjoyed the section of CWA advice relating to stain removal and substitutes for eggs and so on. A sense of pioneering, of making do, of carefully held advice, economy and frugality was strongly present. The experience of self-sufficiency and living in a remote place. Some of that was also in *Little Women*, whose characters were always getting by on nothing, and even perhaps from Pooh and Piglet who would often wander off to see what might turn up. And Pooh was always hungry.

More recently I found an anonymous notebook at a second-hand book sale. It is full of such household lore cut out from newspapers and pasted in alphabetically. Again stain removal was a constant concern. Problems and problem solving. I guess I am looking for ancestors in some way. Self-reliance, old wives' tales, knowledge passed down through the experiences of smell and taste and touch and observation and experience as well as sight. And free or practically free, like herbs and weeds.

23

You read old letters and the faces and voices come back to you. The movies seen, the books read, the words exchanged, the talks and exhibitions, the scents and walks, the expeditions and long nights.

24

What people have to give other people.

25
Excavating the past is like entering a dark cave of fireflies. It consists admittedly mostly of words.

26
Weeding after months of rain is ideal.

27
Things that could be better, things that could be bitter.

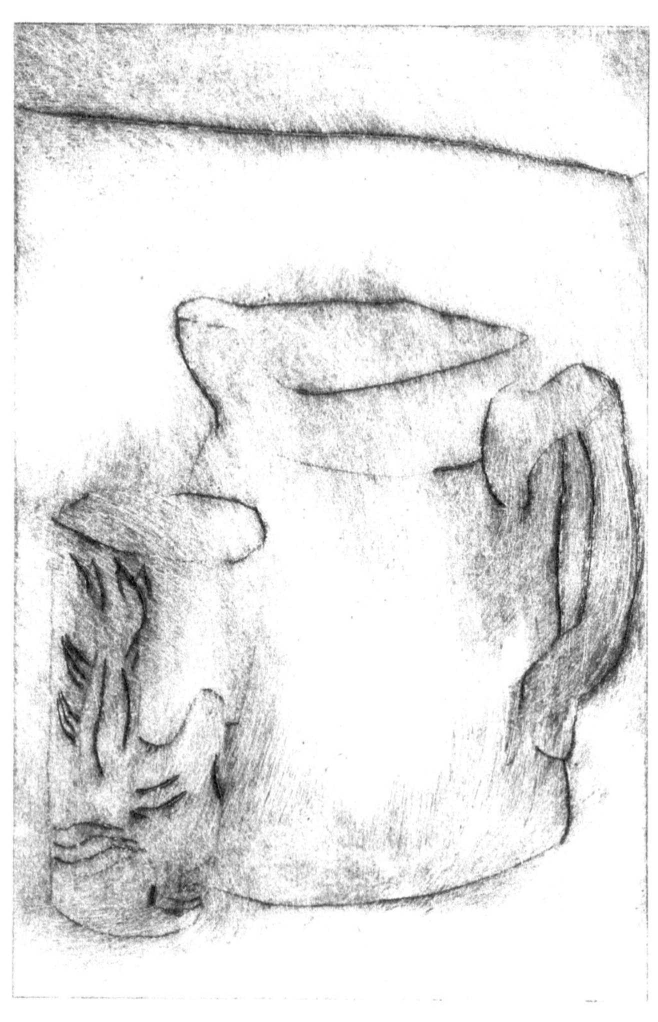

Bird Cup Jug

OCTOBER

3

They say no two blades of grass are alike. People too. How odd.

5

I have a rock collection. Some scientists have given names to all the minerals and forms and substances. In the shape, the texture and the make-up of each is something to hold the hand or the eye – a story, the beginning of a story. A punctuation point. A stripe, an indentation, a flash of another type of rock. So people classify everything and go on and on giving things names and placing them in an order. Is that why we are here? To name and classify the earth and everything on it? I am not convinced.

My rocks sit in drawers sometimes with labels telling the place they were found, their provenance, or else they are arranged on saucers like chocolates. Oxford, Emily Gap, Paris, the Coorong … Their voices take up space and gather dust. Sometimes, rarely rarely, they are washed or if small become companions and go on journeys travelling in my pocket. Some live in a bowl that gets filled with seawater.

They are strong companions, unchanging and stolid, holding a calm demeanour, a patient composure to be emulated and admired. They hold both permanence and transience lightly, keeping one position until moved and then keeping that position. Stacked around the veranda post with shells and coral they keep watch, greet and farewell, hold on, staying still and loyal. They are witnesses.

7

An oracular dream

I enter a concert hall and find my seat. Our block of people is near a school group. We have to move up right near them. I sit next to a lovely young boy who turns out to be a girl and starts giving me things from her pencil case. First she gives me a tiny (key-ring creature size) articulated skeleton. I hold it and unfold it and say thank you. Next is a female standing figure in a dance pose, like a geisha. That is you, she says. Then a bird with a considering eye. I arrange them on a foldout table. We are close. The concert is good. We applaud.

She has a notebook that I see but do not read – just the writing through the back of the paper. I go to find the toilet, it has run out of paper. I get back to my seat and the three objects have gone. I keep looking for them and repeat a description of the three figures in my head again and again so I can recall it when I wake up. Death, the Dancer and the Bird …

12
Wherever something stays still, homes will be built around it.

13
Dream
Helping a young man who needs to be taken to a certain place. A white dog runs up to me for a hug – love. The man must eat a piece of white rope. It's quite long.

16
The DNA we share with trees – 50%, slugs – 70%, cows – 80%, bees – 44%, daffodils – 25%. Roughly 70% with snails too, I guess.

18
Sleeping in, eating quite a bit, a voice from inside my gut seems to comment on what is happening. *Grr, erff, mmm.* Sometimes I call it the commentariat. That almost independent life of the microbiome. Does life have to be so physical?

19
It is good to be still even when walking.

20
I caught a cockroach that was in the microwave. It was spangly like a dog and kicked back, shiny. I grabbed it in a tissue and put it outside in the garden. They never come back.

21
The ghosts of books that were lined up on shelves for years haunt me as colours and spines, titles and names, sensations and ideas.

22
We are all curators.

25
Sitzfleisch. Discipline and continuity.

26
Legendary picnics.

28
Can easily and happily spend an hour a day in the garden. In the absence of humans many other relationships are possible.

30
In the bottle shop some of the staff are dressed for Halloween. My spontaneous laughter at and with one of the witches is free and wide and possesses almost a sense of community.

31
Wakeful night. You are not Patrick White.

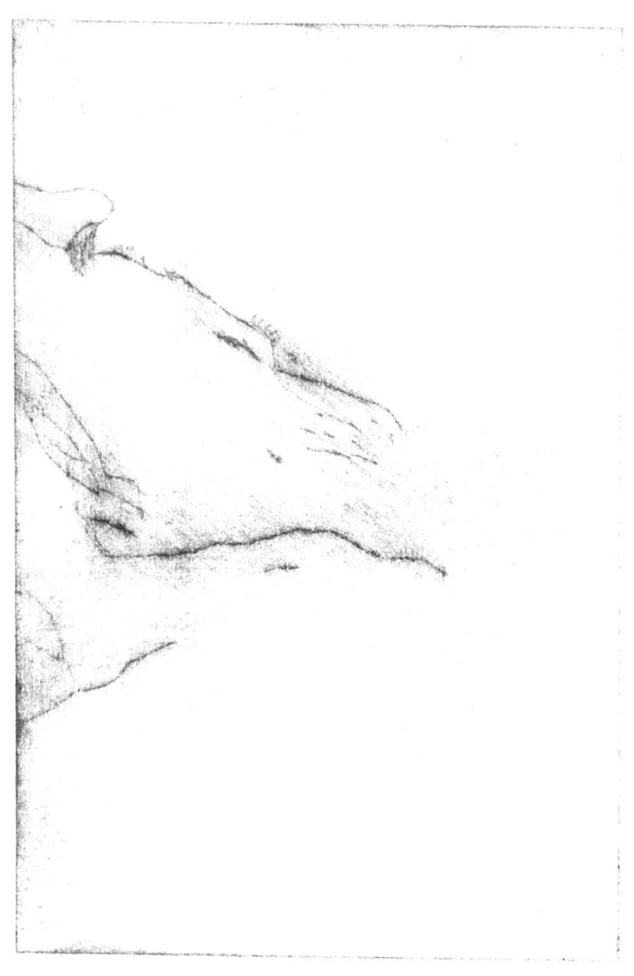

To Dream

NOVEMBER

1
The idea of promise.

2
Slaters are not classified as insects but as crustaceans. A lot of them live in the garden. They gather under things and scurry around when something is moved.

4
Weather – fickle, wild cold raging, sunny and still, still and not sunny, very still.

6
Outside to look at the sky, feel the wind and listen, to crickets starting up in heated and watered earth, see stars and the moon, and a planet shining and blinking out with all colours, red, blue, green, yellow.

7
Two small slugs inside. Carefully with a piece of paper I move them into the garden.

8
Enheduanna – the world's first known author. A woman in Mesopotamia. Of course.

9
A human is like a sewer through which everything passes and is transformed.

11
The cue is taken from drawing. A single line can lead the mind to terraces of contemplation. Ben Okri, *A Time for New Dreams*

12
I can't believe how many books the library deaccessions. Inevitably I bring a lot home.

14
Dissonant archives, the regenerative radical potential of archives.

15
I see a bird flying with a small bird in its claws – food or rescue?

16
A magpie says just try something.

18
The knitting together of body and mind and spirit.

21
A crowd of sulphur-crested cockatoos fly over … calling.

25
A snail can sleep up to three years in a drought. I can imagine doing that.

27
Grilled chicken with yoghourt and sumac-dressed chickpea salad. Olives and blue cheese and celery.

28
Today two skinks are fighting on the front veranda flipping each other aggressively. Eventually one, the younger I think, bites hard into the neck of the other and stuff leaks out. He/she/it holds on firmly … I leave them to it.

29
There's a tree in the corner of my room and a moth somewhere too. The moth is crested and armoured with white. The tree is green and feathery. I have always stood in/near people's gardens and examined their trees.

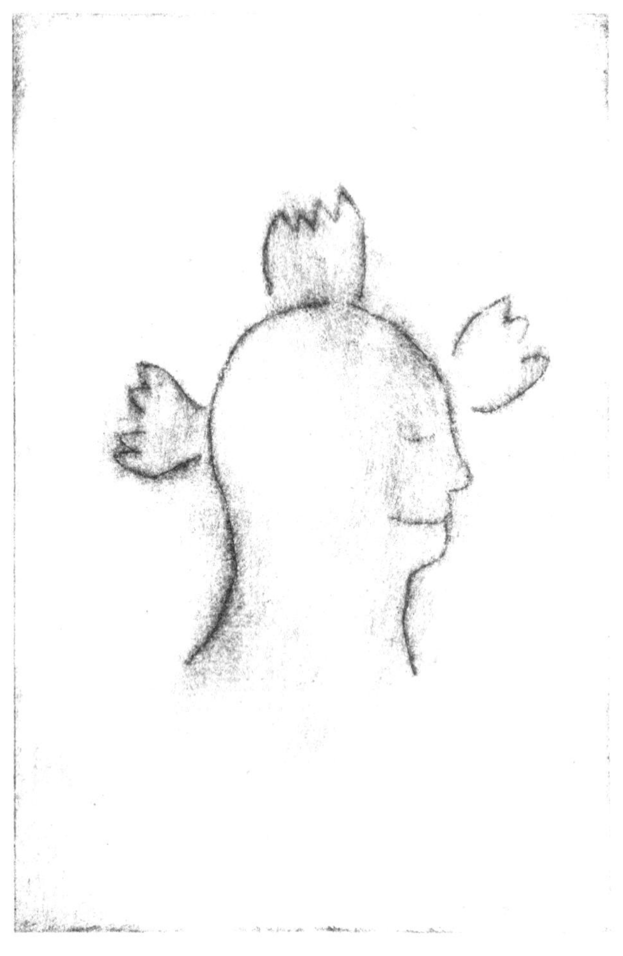

Lady Hetepet sailing across the lotus lake

DECEMBER

1
All my problems are common/ordinary ones. As are all the things that will never be told or said.

2
The scent of the past. Death of a bee. Need a hug.

4
Accidental notes. I once wrote an elaborate description of what they are for a music teacher. It was quite wrong but she was impressed.

6
Dream
A black hippo leading a yoga class (which has just been cancelled and we are all disbelieving). The hippo does a huge piss.

7
Seeking the edges of things.

8
Sometimes I want everything to stop so I can catch up. Full moon, silver, white, black, grey; the air rushes inside when I open the door.

9
In his book *Tell me why* Archie Roach says that he will be there on the other side to greet us all when we get there.

10
Greek for Saturday – lentil salad, mushrooms, zucchini and capsicums à la Grecque, roast vegetables, baked fish, retsina.

12
Dream
Writing on a wall with a blue glitter pen – last word is Hurrah!

It is my contribution. Before that I am walking with a young J by the sea making multiple shallow pools. We run. It is fun. Then we look at a book of outfits we get to choose from. Mine is a brightly coloured kangaroo jacket. He is all in green.

17
She did a lot of nothing.

20
A dragonfly mauled by the cat sat on my hand and then on my shirt for a long time before flying away.

22
Last night in my bedroom a beautiful pale moth sits on me, seems to like me, we talk, then it vanishes. In the morning it flies around the light bulb on the hanging ceiling light and I say if I could catch you I would take you outside. It comes to sit on my arm and I walk it outside where it stays for a while and then flies off towards the sun.

23
Seize the day – if there is one.

24
Cold rolls and chicken soup – very good.

27
Memory – something you go into and something that comes at you.

28
You think you are immortal. Though you know that you are not. You think you have all the time in the world to lie around and dream and sleep. You like the enforced inactivity of sleep, the quietness, the lack of demands, the silence, the deafness, the oblivion. And seeing friends and family in odd situations.

So you may even enjoy death as it resembles sleep so much, except it is cold, very cold. No one including yourself will expect you to do anything once you are dead. You will be released from all ambition and longing and fear and desire and sorrow and unkindness.

Zbigniew Herbert in his prose poem *Episode in a Library* sees someone copying out a poem in shorthand and sees that what we leave behind are just marks on paper.

> *A blonde girl is bent over a poem. With a pencil sharp as a lancet she transfers the words to a blank page and changes them into strokes, accents, caesuras. The lament of a fallen poet now looks like a salamander eaten away by ants.*
> *When we carried him away under machine-gun fire, I believed that his still warm body would be resurrected in the word. Now as I watch the death of the words, I know there is no limit to decay. All that will be left after us in the black earth will be scattered syllables. Accents over nothingness and dust.*

But maybe also good recipes, fond memories, and delight in what is light, like clouds, hats and butterflies. And let's face it, lots of rubbish … oh dear.

29

I am a citizen of the world and my nationality is good will. Socrates

30

J wants to remake the world. While he is away I think of a hundred things to tell him.

31

Once I was as light as air, as light as air.

Author's Note

Under the Bed and *Inventory 2020* were first published in *HEAT* magazine, respectively in Series 3 Number 5, 2022, and Series 3 Number 12, 2023.

I would like to acknowledge the enthusiasm and attention to detail of *HEAT*'s then editor Alexandra Christie.

A fragment of *Under the Bed* was used in the HSC NSW English Advanced Examination 2023.

Inventory 2020 and *Inventory 2022* are accompanied by Radok's etchings *The Everyday Suite* 2024. *Inventory 2021* is accompanied by *The Pre-Columbian Suite* etchings that she made in 2008. Their titles are Spanish proverbs.

I would like to acknowledge the resilience and encouragement of Michael Bollen and the thoughtful editing of Julia Beaven.

And the generosity and love of my family and friends.

www.ingramcontent.com/pod-product-compliance
Ingram Content Group Australia Pty Ltd
76 Discovery Rd, Dandenong South VIC 3175, AU
AUHW010951010825
414680AU00004B/4

9 781923 388024